AF580458

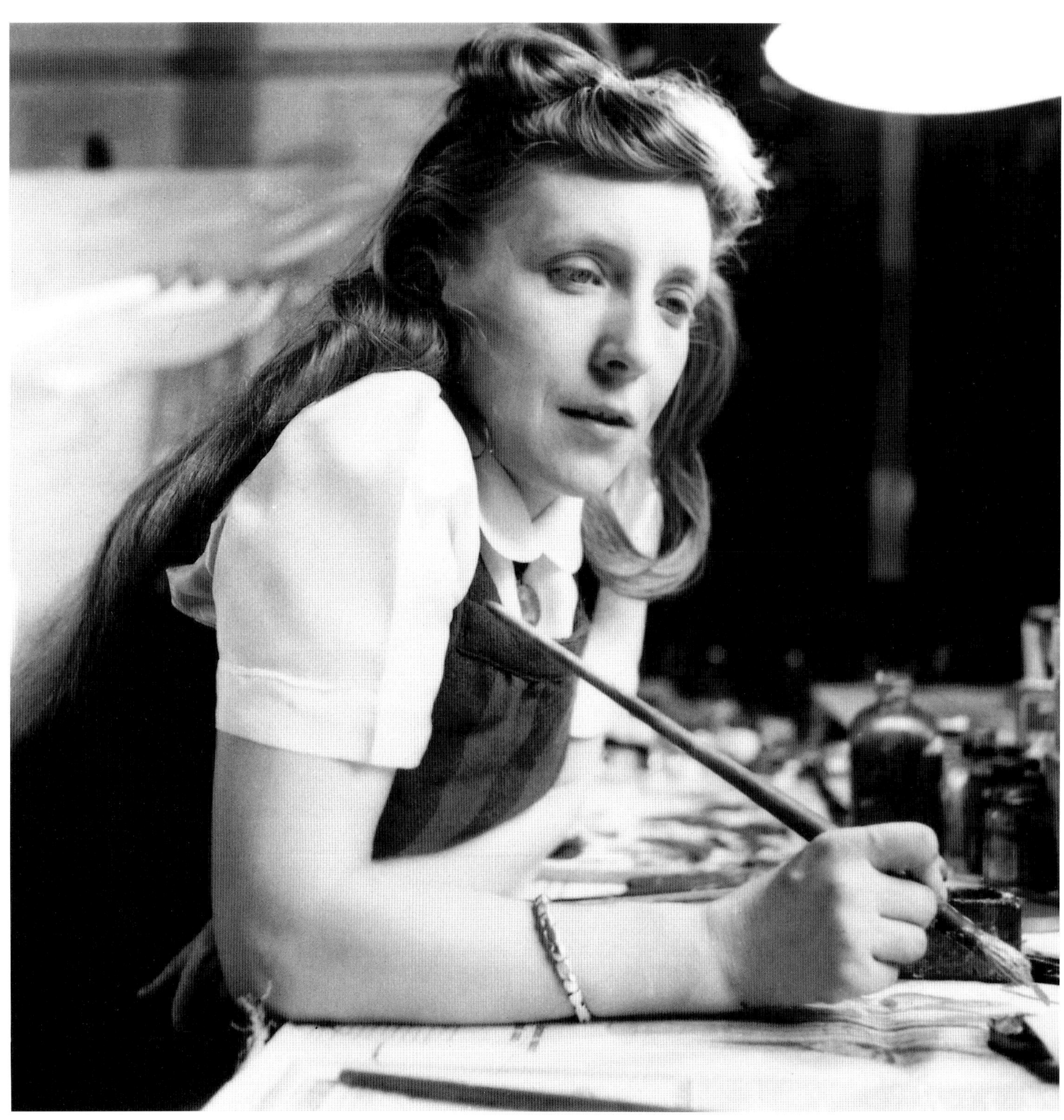

Louise Bourgeois, ca. 1946

Thomas Kellein

Louise Bourgeois

Kunsthalle Bielefeld 1999

Zweibändiger Katalog zur Ausstellung »Louise Bourgeois. Spinnen, Einzelgänger, Paare« in der Kunsthalle Bielefeld vom 28. 2. bis 2. 5.1999.

Band I: Skulpturen 1994–1998. Band II: Die Zeichnungen 1996–1998.

Die Kunsthalle dankt Louise Bourgeois, Jerry Gorovoy und Wendy Williams sehr herzlich für Rat und Unterstützung bei der Ausstellung und den beiden Publikationen. Der Dank gilt ebenfalls für die Leihgeberinnen und Leihgeber aus Deutschland, der Schweiz, Italien und den USA.

Two-volume catalogue for the exhibition *Louise Bourgeois. Spinnen, Einzelgänger, Paare/Spiders, Singletons, Couples*, at the Kunsthalle Bielefeld, from 28 February to 2 May 1999.

Volume I: Sculptures 1994–1998. Volume II: The Drawings 1996–1998.

The Kunsthalle warmly thanks Louise Bourgeois, Jerry Gorovoy and Wendy Williams for advice and support in the preparation of the exhibition and of both catalogue volumes. Thanks also to the lenders in Germany, Switzerland, Italy and the USA.

Die Deutsche Bibliothek – CIP-Einheitsaufnahme

Louise Bourgeois: Kunsthalle Bielefeld 1999; [zweibandiger Katalog zur Austellung »Louise Bourgeois, Spinnen, Einzelgänger, Paare« in der Kunsthalle Bielefeld vom 28.2. bis 2.5. 1999]/Thomas Kellein.
[Übers.: David Britt], – Köln: König

ISBN 3-88375-363-7

Bd. 2. Die Zeichnungen 1996–1998.

Layout: Hansjörg Mayer, London

Übersetzung/Translations: David Britt, London

Lithos/Litho organisation: Repro Mayer, Reutlingen

Druck und Herstellung/Print and Production: Druckerei Cantz, Ostfildern

Distribution: Buchhandlung Walther König, Köln

Auflage/Print run: 2.000 Exemplare

ISBN: 3-88375-363-7

© Kunsthalle Bielefeld und der Autor für Text und Layout.
Louise Bourgeois Studio für alle Werke und Abbildungen

Kunsthalle Bielefeld and the author for text and layout
Louise Bourgeois Studio for all works and reproductions

Printed in Germany

Die Zeichnungen von 1996–1998

The Drawings from 1996 - 1998

Das künstlerische Geheimnis von Louise Bourgeois liegt weder in ihrer Angst noch in den lesenswerten, vielfach brillanten Erklärungen zu ihrer Arbeit. Es hat mehr mit einer tief ausgeprägten, reflexiven Wachsamkeit und ihrem besonders assoziativen Vorgehen zu tun.

Ihr zeichnerisches Werk entwickelt sich oft aus physisch impulsiven Strichsetzungen, als gingen die Motive nicht vom Kopf, sondern von einem Grundgerüst aus Linien und Koordinaten aus. Patterns, Scribbles, Kreise, Spiralen oder Ansätze von Treppen bedecken vielfach ein Blatt zuerst. Spontan hingeworfene Figuren und Kompositionen gibt es dafür nur in Ausnahmefällen. Die Zeichnungen entwickeln sich langsam und stetig. Nie sind sie auf Anhieb fertig. Es ist nicht zwingend, daß sich aus einem solch heuristischen Sammeln visueller Elemente sogleich ein Kraftfeld ergibt. Aber Tag für Tag, manchmal in den Morgenstunden, vor allem aber am Abend und nachts, entstehen und entwickeln sich Konfigurationen, die eine starke Ordnungs- und Kommunikationstendenz erkennen lassen. »Mein ganzes Leben ist wie ein Metronom organisiert«, hat sie erst vor wenigen Jahren gesagt.[1]

Das beständige Interesse an visuellen Phänomenen, die häufige Interferenz von Erinnerungen und verbalen Phantasien sowie vor allem die hohe Arbeitsdisziplin bilden das Rückgrat eines zeichnerischen Oeuvres, das vor allem Beziehungen abbildet. Das Geheimnisvolle konstituiert sich nicht durch Virtuosität, sondern in meist unerwarteten Querverbindungen eines begonnenen Motivfelds mit anderen Elementen. Eine homogene Kritzelei wirkt plötzlich ambivalent, eine zunächst einfache Arbeit führt zur Zwei-, Drei- oder Mehrgesichtigkeit eines Gegenstands. Am Ende stehen Vexierbilder - jedoch ohne vordergründige Sensation. Eine Kunst, die man mit dem Auge wie eine Ansammlung heterogener Charaktere oder wie ein Haus mit nicht zusammengehörigen Zimmern erfährt. Es gibt thematische Schwerpunkte und inhaltliche Zielrichtungen – wie in jüngster Zeit das Thema Haus oder eine fast asiatische Vorliebe für Füße.

Gerne verwendet sie Notenpapier, um auf bereits vorhandenen Strukturen aufzubauen. Diese werden zum Beispiel mit Hausformen aus einem Viereck und einem Dreieck gefüllt (s. S. 11). Am Anfang kann die Frage nach der Größenrelation beider Formen stehen. Die Häuser in der zweiten Reihe definieren sich dann nicht mehr durch die Größe, sondern durch ihre Stellung zueinander. Ein halbes Haus und ein schiefes Haus am Bildrand sorgen für eine erste Störung des eben begonnenen Systems. Der nächste Arbeitsschritt legt ein weiteres Thema nahe, das in der Dominanz einzelner Häuser vor anderen oder in ihrer Gruppierung neben der Vereinzelung bestehen kann. Nach vorne zum unteren Blattrand hin ist unabhängig davon ein überproportionales Wachstum von Häusern aufgrund einer veränderteren Perspektive zu erkennen, so daß das Blatt voll geworden ist, ohne ein greifbares Resultat zu zeigen.

Andere Hausdarstellungen deuten kasernenartige Siedlungen und ihre Verkabelung mit Menschen, Wegen oder unterirdischen Kanälen an. Die Häuser selbst mögen wie Hütten oder

The secret of Louise Bourgeois' art lies neither in her fear nor in the readable and sometimes brilliant explanations that she gives of her work. It has more to do with a deeply ingrained, reflective alertness and with her specific, associative working method.

Her drawings often evolve from impulsive patterns of strokes, as if the motifs did not come from the head but from a basic scaffolding of lines and coordinates. First, a leaf is covered with patterns, scribbles, circles, spirals or the beginnings of staircases. Spontaneous jottings of figures and compositions occur only in exceptional cases. The drawings evolve slowly and steadily. They are never finished immediately. This kind of heuristic collection of visual elements does not necessarily generate a force field at once. But day after day, sometimes in the mornings, but mostly in the evenings and nights, configurations appear and evolve that reveal a strong tendency to create order and communication. 'My whole life is organized like a metronome,' she said a few years ago.[1]

Her constant interest in visual phenomena, the frequent intrusion of memories and verbal fantasies into her work, and above all its superior discipline, form the background of a body of drawings that serves above all to illustrate connections. The mysterious takes shape not through virtuosity but through cross-references (mostly unexpected) from one emergent motivic field to another. A homogeneous scribble suddenly looks ambivalent; an initially simple work leads to an object with two, three, or more layers of meaning. Superficially unsensational, these are puzzle pictures. This is an art that the eye experiences as a collection of heterogeneous characters, or as a house with rooms that do not belong together. There are recurrent motifs and thematic centres – most recently, the house theme, or an almost Asiatic predilection for feet.

She likes to use music manuscript paper, in order to build upon pre-existent structures. These are, for instance, filled with house forms made up of a rectangle and a triangle (see p. 11). It may all begin with the issue of the relative sizes of these two forms. The houses in the second row then no longer define themselves through their size but through their relative positions. The system is no sooner begun than it is disrupted by a half-house and a crooked house at the edge of the image. The next step is to introduce an additional theme: either the dominance of some houses over others, or the juxtaposition of grouping with isolation. Independently, a modified perspective causes the same houses to be disproportionately enlarged towards the lower, near edge of the image; and so the sheet is filled without yielding any tangible outcome.

Other images of houses hint at barrack-like housing estates, linked by the human figure, by paths, or by underground conduits. In the last few years, Bourgeois has shown these as if they were not dwellings but merely containers. They testify to her constant interest in the interchange between inside and outside.

As for feet, the eye falls upon shoes and then on the foot inside

gar wie Hüte sein. Bourgeois hat sie in den letzten Arbeitsjahren nicht so sehr als Wohnungen, sondern als schlichte Container aufgefaßt. Sie signalisieren das ständige Hin und Her zwischen Innen und Außen.

Bei den Füßen fällt der Blick auf Schuhe und den Fuß darin. Damenpumps mit halbhohen Absätzen sind mit sichtbar nackten Füßen und Zehen gefüllt. Wie ein Dach zieht sich ein Kind einen Schuh über den Kopf. Wie ein Haus erscheint ein anderer Schuh – durch zwei Türen und acht Fenster – betretbar. Schuhe können auch, durch verschiedene Größen, Simulanten für Familiensituationen sein.

Die Fußsohlen wiederum nutzt Bourgeois als Gesichtsfeld. Beide Füße suggerieren eine Nähe zur Symmetrie unserer Augen, wobei Nase und Mund zwischen die Füße fallen. Eine Fußsohle kann auch den Schwung einer wohlproportionierten Kopfpartie suggerieren.

Eine Dreiergruppe von Zeichnungen auf Notenpapier (S. 32–34) beginnt spontan ein neues Thema, wobei sich das erste Blatt auf den Violinschlüssel, zweimal den Baßschlüssel und je eine dazugehörige Note beschränkt. Die drei Motive flottieren im Raum, die Musik schwebt bei Louise Bourgeois sozusagen in der Luft. Auch hier haben sich Assoziationen niedergeschlagen, die als Resümee ohne eindeutiges Fazit bleiben. Das zweite Blatt stellt die Tonleiter vor: ansteigend in Form von dicken Punkten, analog zu den schwarzen Tasten auf der Klaviatur. Aus den Punkten werden oben Rhythmen mit Synkopen – doch zu wirklicher Musik kommt es wiederum nicht. Das dritte Blatt, von dem man eine Konklusion erwarten könnte, verläßt wiederum das System (noch ehe es recht begonnen hat), indem der Violinschlüssel durch zwei eingezeichnete Augen die Rolle eines Beobachters einnimmt und sein Gegenstück, den Baßschlüssel, als einen Fuß beäugt, an den ein Stein geworfen wurde. Die Steine setzen sich am unteren Bildrand in Form von kleinen Herzen fort. Das Blatt ist recto »La blessure au pied« (Die Fußverletzung) betitelt. Hat die Schwere einer unwillkürlich heraufziehenden Erinnerung so über die anfängliche Absicht der Zeichnung gesiegt?

Schon nach zwei oder drei Zeichnungen fällt auf, daß Rot die Grundfarbe ist. Es ist das Rot von Kugelschreibern und Filzstiften. Gelegentlich wird Bleistift zur Vorzeichnung eingesetzt. Ist das Resultat besonders ansehnlich, in den Augen der Bourgeois »fertig«, wird das Blatt mit blauen Tönen bereichert und gelegentlich vollflächig hinterlegt.

Wie eine Wiese ist ein blaues Feld dekoriert (S. 40), auf dem rote kreisförmige Blüten durch rote Schnüre verbunden sind, von denen rote Kugeln herabhängen. Es kann eine Girlande sein, vielleicht aber auch ein Weg mit Bäumen, zwischen denen Laternen baumeln. Bei den schwarzen Blütenstempeln ist das Papier nach hinten durchstochen. Der Versuch, aus Kreislinien und Spiralen ein motivisches Netz zu erschaffen, führt in diesem Fall (S. 41) zu einem setzkastenähnlichen Dekor, das an Gustav Klimt erinnert. Eine rote Filzstiftlinie hält alle Figuren zusammen wie der Ring an einem Korb. Das blaue Quadrat und

them. Ladies' pumps with semi-high heels are filled with visibly bare feet and toes. A child pulls a shoe over its head like a roof. In another drawing, a shoe with two doors and eight windows looks as if you could walk into it, like a house. Shoes of differing sizes may also stand in for family situations.

Again, Bourgeois uses the soles of feet as faces. Two feet recall the symmetry of eyes, with nose and mouth between. A single sole may suggest the curve of a well-proportioned head.

A group of three drawings on music paper (pp. 32–34) spontaneously takes up a new theme. The first sheet contains nothing but one treble clef and two bass clefs, each followed by a single note. The three motifs float in space: music hangs in the air. Associations intrude here too, summarized but not summed up. The second drawing shows a scale, ascending in the form of fat dots, like the black keys on a keyboard. Above, the dots become rhythms with syncopations – but still no real music. The third drawing, which might be expected to provide a conclusion, abandons the system before it has really got started. The treble clef acquires two eyes and takes on the role of a spectator, eyeing its opposite number, the bass clef, which takes the form of a foot with a stone dropped on it. The stones continue along the lower edge in the form of little hearts. On the recto, the sheet bears the title 'La blessure au pied' (the foot injury). Has the weight of an involuntary memory prevailed over the initial intention of the drawing?

After the first two or three drawings, it begins to be apparent that the basic colour here is red. This is the red of ballpoint pens and felt tips. Sometimes pencil is used for the initial drawing. When the outcome is particularly good, and Bourgeois regards it as 'finished', it is enriched with blue tones and sometimes given an all-over background.

A blue field is decorated like a meadow (p. 40), and on it red, cruciform flowers are linked by red cords from which red balls depend. Perhaps this is a garland, or else a path lined by trees with lanterns strung between them. The flowers are black stamps, and these have made holes in the paper. In another example (p. 41) the attempt to create a motivic network from rings and spirals leads to a décor of rectangular compartments, like a type-case; the effect is reminiscent of Gustav Klimt. A red felt-tip line holds all the figures together, like a ring on a basket. The blue square and the blue circle restore a balance – not that the system has been particularly disturbed.

In two black and white drawings (see both covers), done in July 1998, Bourgeois refers back to the sculpture *Dagger Child* (1947–49). This consisted of four closely fitted layers of wood in the shape of a dagger. The first drawing shows a crying child with arms raised, evidently looking at a sea of smoke and flames. On the reverse of the same sheet (back cover vol. I), is the title: *The Punishment of the Dagger Child*. A string of other notes, also on the reverse, reads as follows: 'The destruction of the mother. The dagger. Messerschmidt. Fuselli [Fuseli]. Prudhon. La justice hoursur [?] au . . . [?] Pauvre crime. La Matricide. Nancy Friday. La Rivière no . . . [?] de la rage haine. Si

der blaue Kreis sorgen in diesem Ensemble für Ausgleich, ohne daß das System sonderlich gestört worden wäre.

Mit zwei schwarzen Zeichnungen (Umschlagabbildungen Bd. I u. II)), die im Juli 1998 entstanden sind, greift sie auf die Skulptur »Dagger Child« von 1947-49 zurück. Diese bestand aus vier eng aneinanderliegenden Holzschichten in Dolchform. Die Zeichnungen zeigen im ersten Fall ein schreiendes Kind mit erhobenen Armen, das offenbar ein Meer aus Rauch und Flammen vor sich sieht. Rückseitig ist es (Rückumschlag Bd. I) »The punishment of the Dagger Child« betitelt. Eine Reihe weiterer umseitiger Notizen lautet: »The destruction of the mother. The dagger. Messerschmidt. Fuselli (d.i. Füssli). Prudhon. La justice hoursur au...(?). Pauvre crime. La Matricide. Nancy Friday. La Rivière no ... de la rage haine. Si elle s'approche, je vais la tuer. La lave brûlante du ..esure. Elle envahit tout sur son chemin, elle engloutie tout à marée haute.« Beim zweiten Blatt stecken drei der Skulptur »Dagger Child« verwandte Dolche in einer liegenden, anscheinend schlafenden Figur. Es könnte die Mutter sein. »The dagger child hurt the parent« ist recto zu lesen. Wie Blitze, wie Lava stellen beide Zeichnungen Bourgeois' altes Thema dar: Wie der Mord an Mutter und Vater tiefes Entsetzen, tiefe Bestürzung und zugleich die von Lucy Lippard einmal »stoische Ruhe« genannte Stimmung erzeugt.

»Miss Moody« (Fräulein Trübsal) (S. 47) heißt eine Arbeit noch von 1997, die ursprünglich von Bleistiftzackenlinien ausging. Aus den etwa parallel verlaufenden Lineamenten sind durch rote Überzeichnungen kleine Gebirgszüge entstanden, deren blau schraffierte Gipfel eine Frau mit wehendem Haar gelockt zu haben scheinen. Die Gipfel werden von ihr mit den Händen berührt. Sie ist nackt, trägt aber Stöckelschuhe. Daß ihr Unterleib auf einer der Spitzen aufliegt, scheint sienicht zu irritieren. Vielleicht ist die Person aufgrund ihrer »Launen« schwerelos geworden. Hier erscheint lieblich und verspielt, was auf anderen Blättern grausam und blutig wirkt.

»Wenn man etwas zu verstecken hat, kommen die Haare zu Hilfe«, hat Bourgeois zu einer ihrer früheren Zeichnungen, die eine Frau mit besonders langen Haaren zeigt, gesagt.[2] Das vorliegende Blatt (Umschlag Bd. II) (s. Titelabbildung) sollte ursprünglich anders aussehen: Der Kopf der Frau war in Höhe des Dekolletées angelegt, die Arme luden weiter aus. Die jetzige, hochgestreckte Mutter mit offenem Mund ist ein Mischwesen geworden. Ihre Haare hängen bis zum Boden, so daß die Strähnen von einem Kind wie die Zweige eines Busches umfaßt werden können. Zugleich quellen Haare auch aus ihrem Mund. Sie hat keine Arme (für Bourgeois herkömmlicherweise immer ein Zeichen von Hilflosigkeit), und ihr Körper mit tief hängenden, großen Brüsten flieht so stark nach oben und unten, daß die kleinen Füße (mit Stöckelschuhen) mit dem Fehlen des Gesichts Regungslosigkeit und schicksalhaftes Festgewurzeltsein signalisieren. Rückseitig sind folgende Satzfetzen zu lesen: »Vas-y ou vous sérez violée comme un lapin vide. Femme à rayures. The bad mother with the small self portrait«.

elle s'approche, je vais la tuer. La lave brûlante du ... esure. Elle envahie tout sur son chemin, ell engloutie tout à marée haute.' [... Justice ... Poor crime. The mother-killer. Nancy Friday. The river ... of rage hate. If she comes any closer, I'll kill her. The burning lava of ... She invades everything in her path, she devours everything at high tide.] On the second sheet, three daggers related to the sculpture *Dagger Child* have been plunged into a reclining, apparently sleeping figure. This might be the mother. 'The dagger child hurts the parent' is the inscription on the recto. Like lightning, like lava, other drawings present Bourgeois' oldest theme: how the murder of father and mother arouses deep horror, deep grief and also what Lucy Lippard once called 'stoic calm'.

Miss Moody (p. 47) is the title of a work dating from 1997, which originated in jagged pencil lines. A red overdrawing has turned the original, roughly parallel lines into tiny mountain ranges, whose blue crosshatched summits seem to hold an attraction for a woman with flowing hair. She touches the mountaintops with her hands. She is naked except for high-heeled shoes. Her lower abdomen rests on one of the sharp points, but this does not seem to bother her. Perhaps her 'moods' have made her weightless. All that appears in other drawings as cruel and bloodthirsty, this drawing turns to prettiness and play.

'When you have something to hide, hair comes to the rescue,' said Bourgeois apropos of one of her earlier drawings, which shows a woman with exceptionally long hair.[2] The present drawing (see cover Voll. II) was originally meant to look quite different; the woman's head was placed level with her décolleté, and she had arms spread wide. The present figure of a mother stretching up, with mouth open, is a hybrid. Her hair hangs down to the floor, so that a child can clasp the strands like the branches of a bush. At the same time, hairs sprout from her mouth. She has no arms (traditionally a sign of helplessness in Bourgeois' work), and her body with its big, pendulous breasts tapers so markedly above and below that the little feet (in high heels) serve in the absence of a face to signal immobility and a fateful state of rootedness. On the reverse are fragmentary phrases: 'Vas-y ou vous serez violée comme un lapin vide. Femme à rayures. [Get on, or you'll be raped like a drawn rabbit. Striped woman.] The bad mother with the small self portrait.'

[1] Louise Bourgeois. *Destruction of the Father. Reconstruction of the Father. Writings and Interviews 1923–1997.* Edited and with texts by Marie-Laure Bernadac and Hans-Ulrich Obrist. London 1998, p. 313.
[2] Ebd./ibid., p. 296.

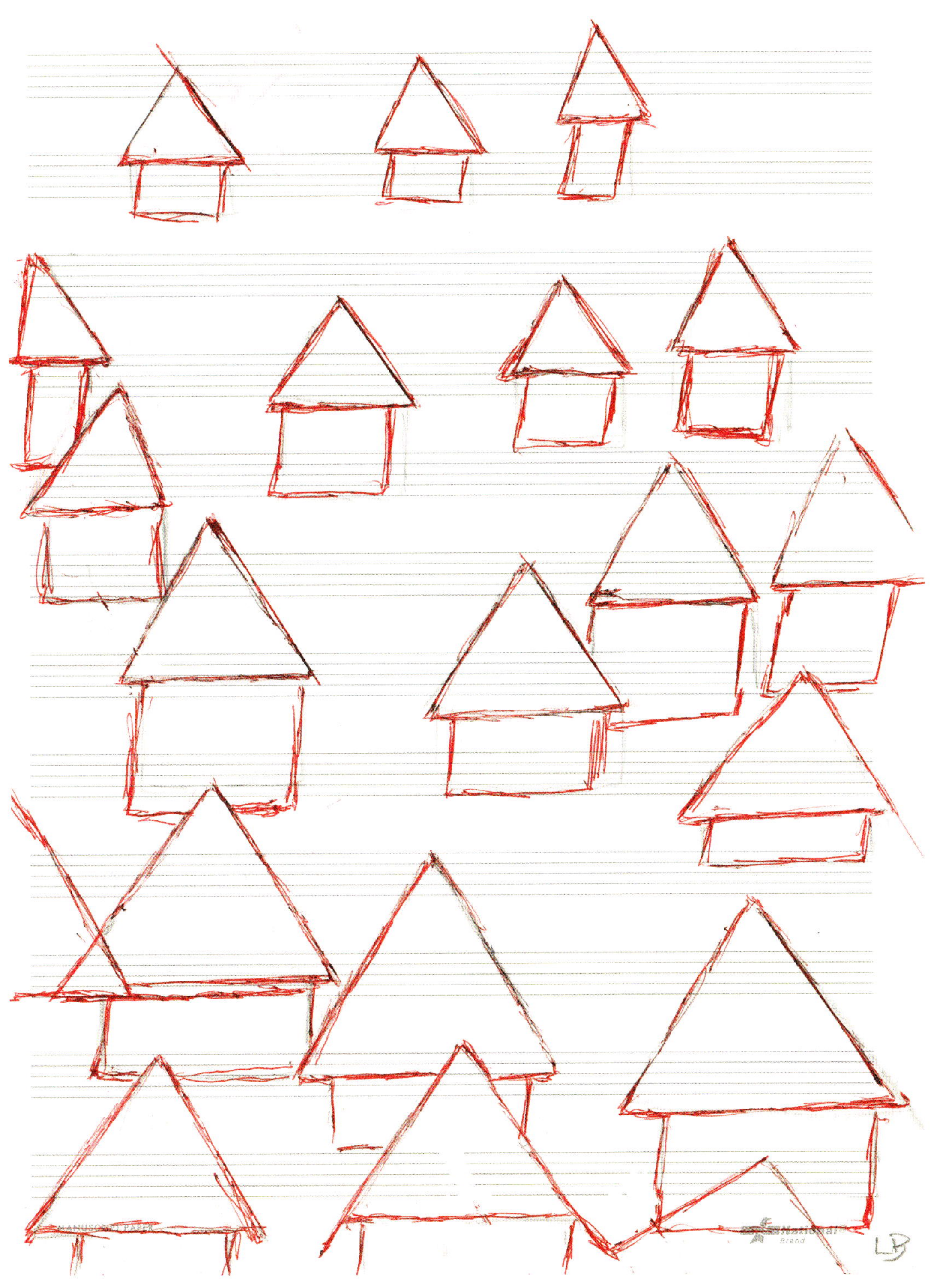

Ohne Titel/Untitled, 1997
Rote Tinte, weisse Gouache und Kohle auf Papier/
Red Ink, White Gouache and Charcoal on Paper, 30 x 21 cm

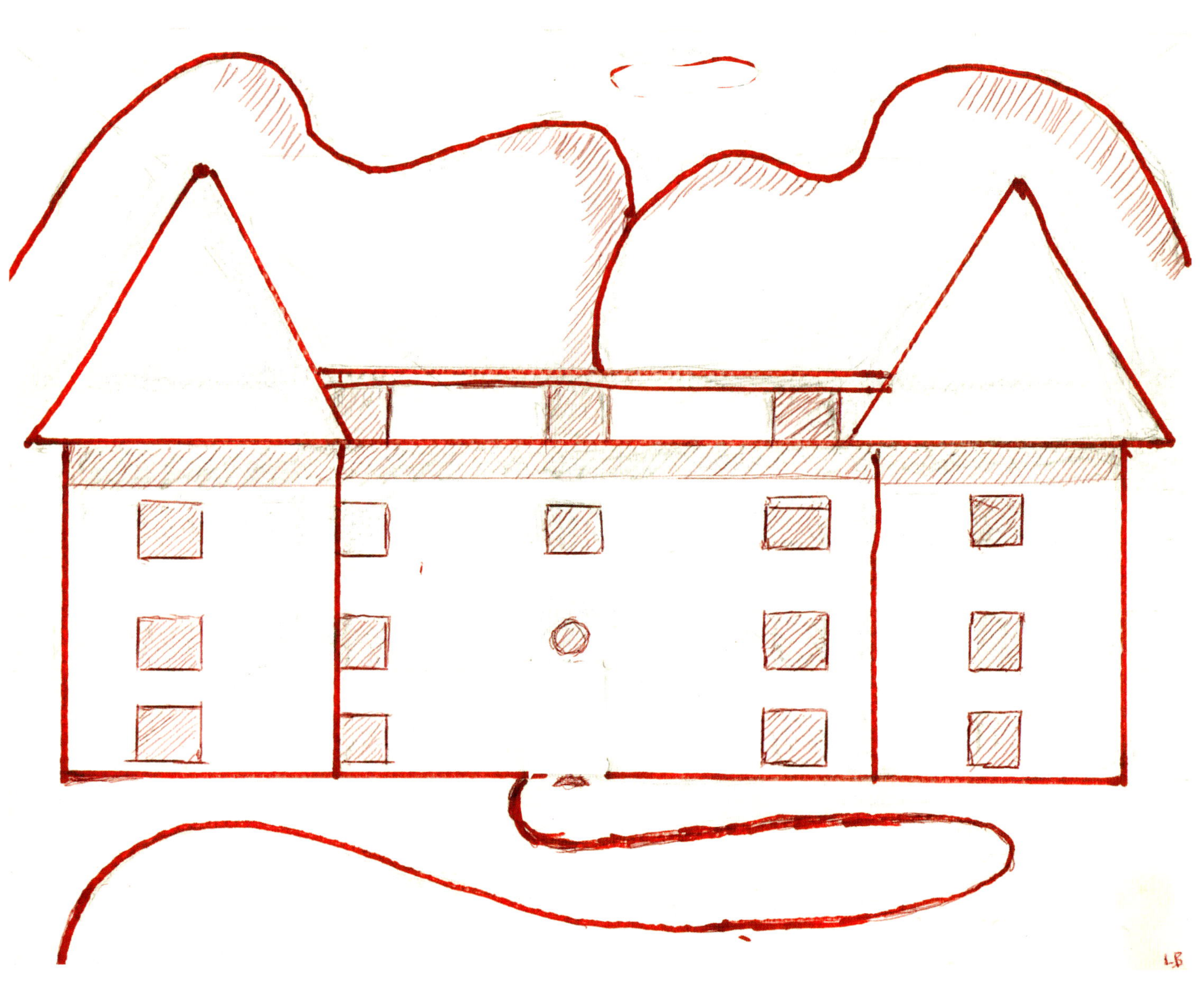

Ohne Titel/Untitled, 1997
Rote Tinte, Bleistift und Ausschnitte auf Papier/
Red Ink, Pencil and Cutouts on Paper, 23 x 30 cm

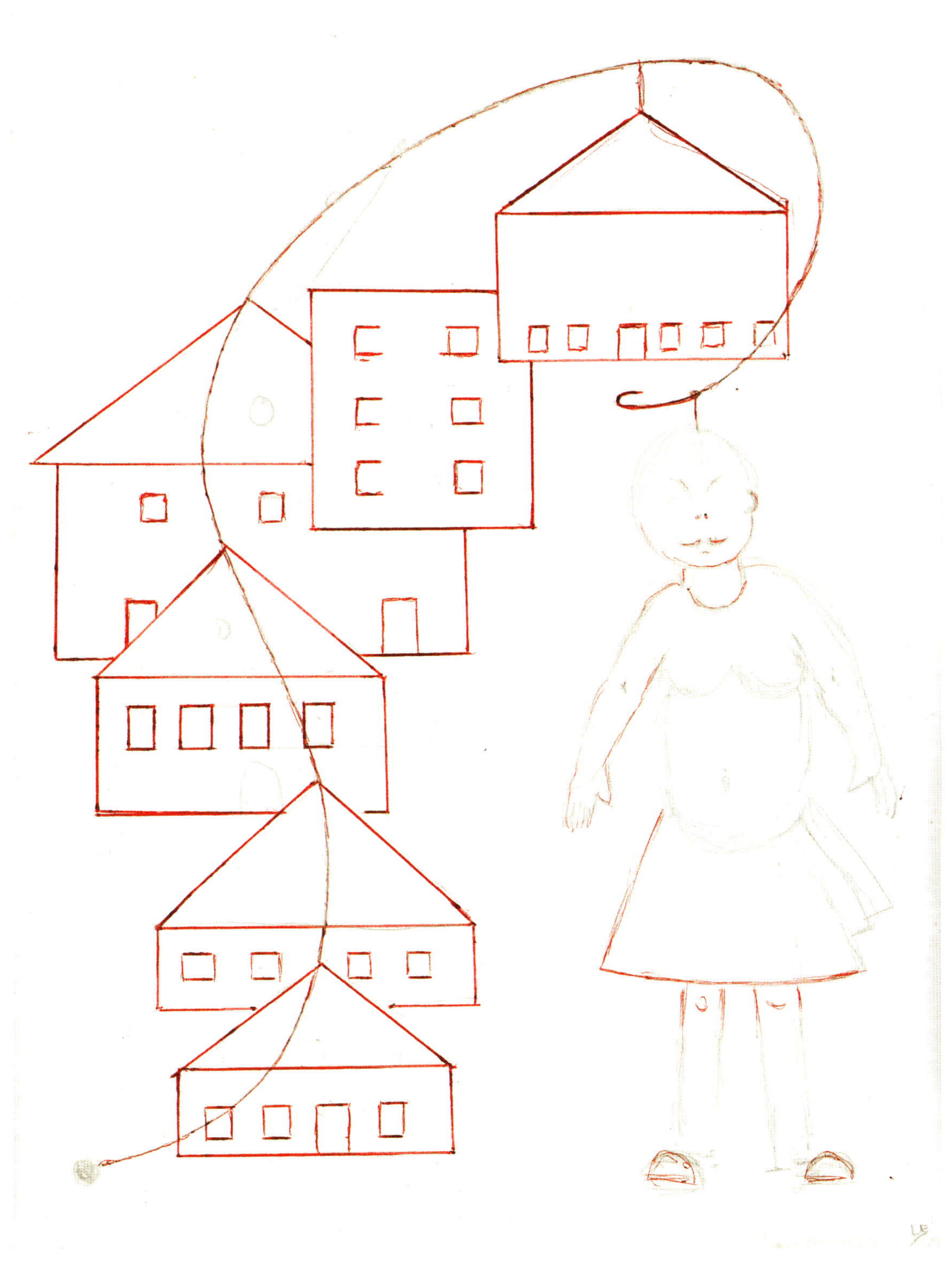

Ohne Titel/Untitled, 1997
Rote Tinte und Bleistift auf Papier/
Red Ink and Pencil on Paper, 30 x 23 cm

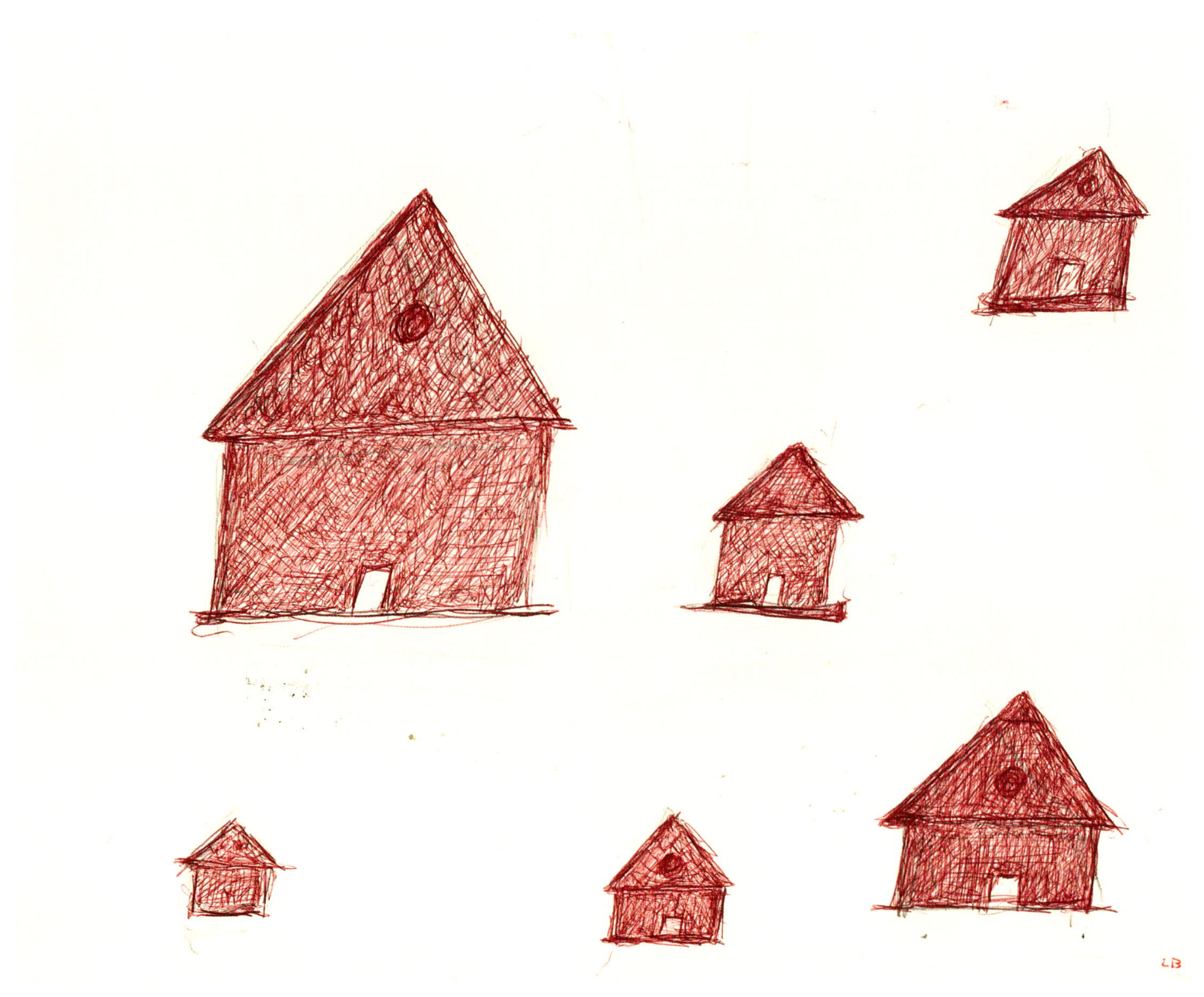

Ohne Titel/Untitled, 1998
Rote Tinte und Bleistift auf Papier/
Red Ink and Pencil on Paper, 23 x 29 cm

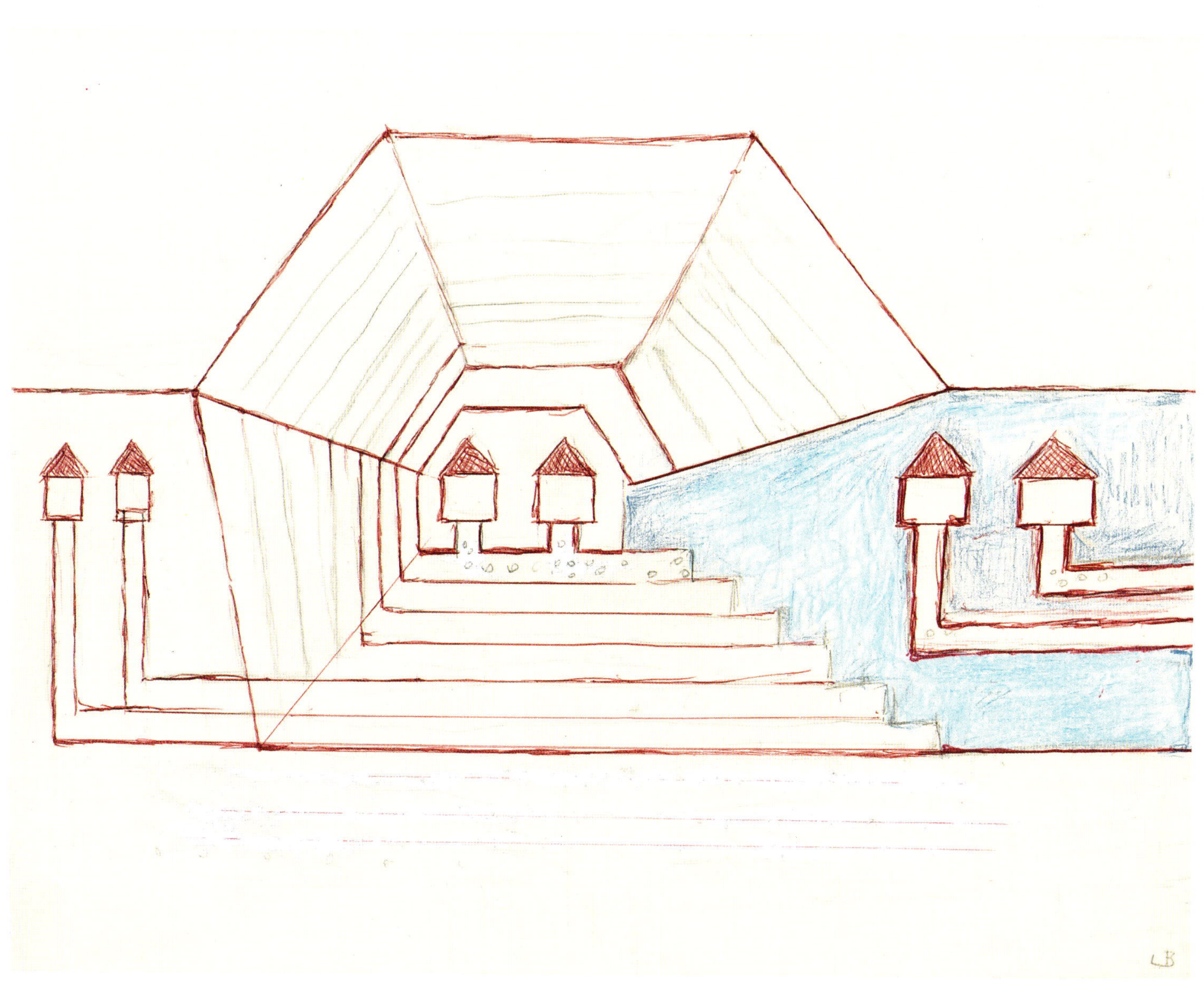

System of Exits, 1998
Rote Tinte, blauer Pastellstift, Bleistift und weisse Gouache auf Papier/
Red Ink, Blue Crayon, Pencil and White Gouache on Paper, 23 x 30 cm

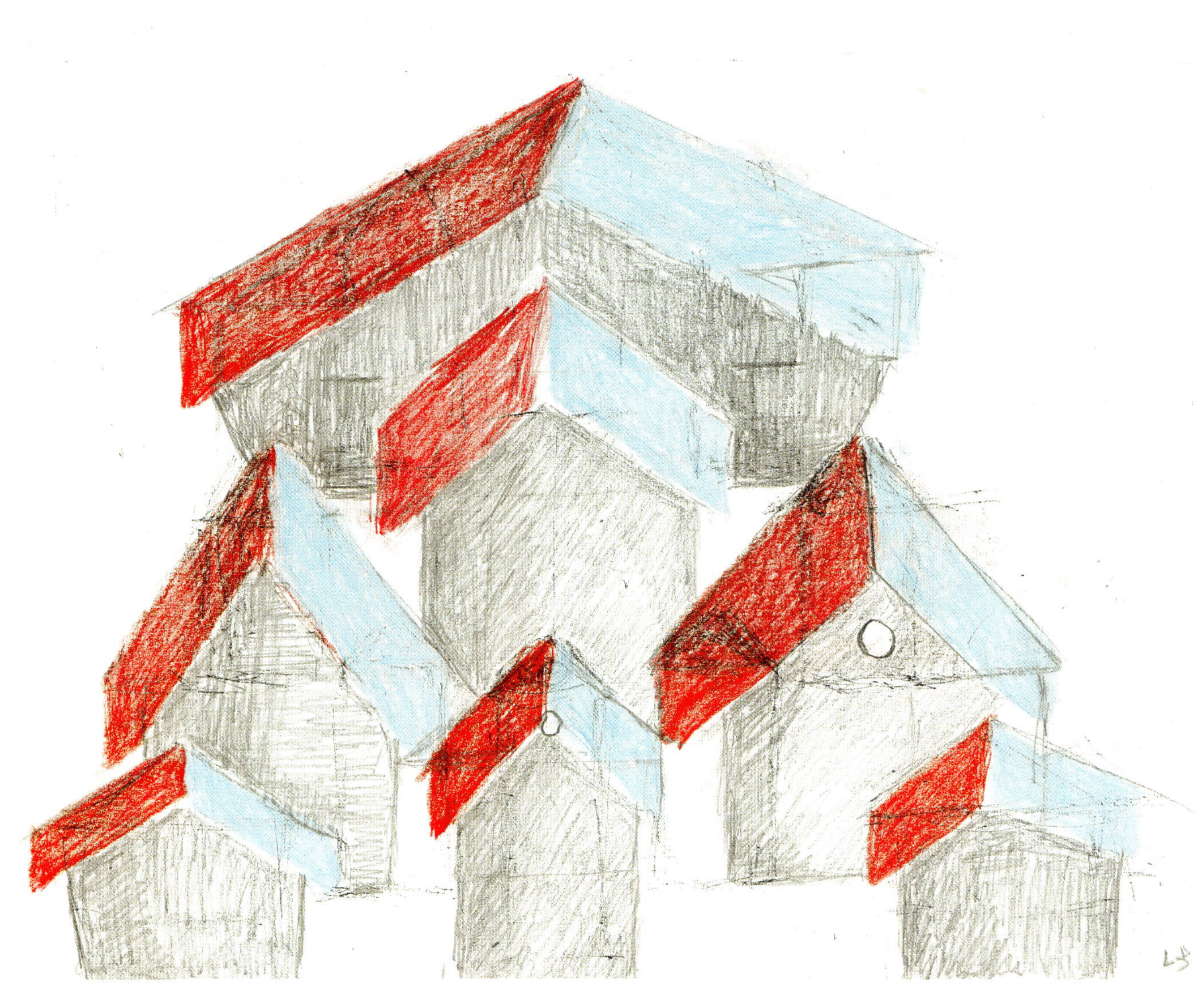

Ohne Titel/Untitled, 1997
Roter und blauer Pastellstift und Bleistift auf Papier/
Red and Blue Crayon and Pencil on Paper, 23 x 30 cm

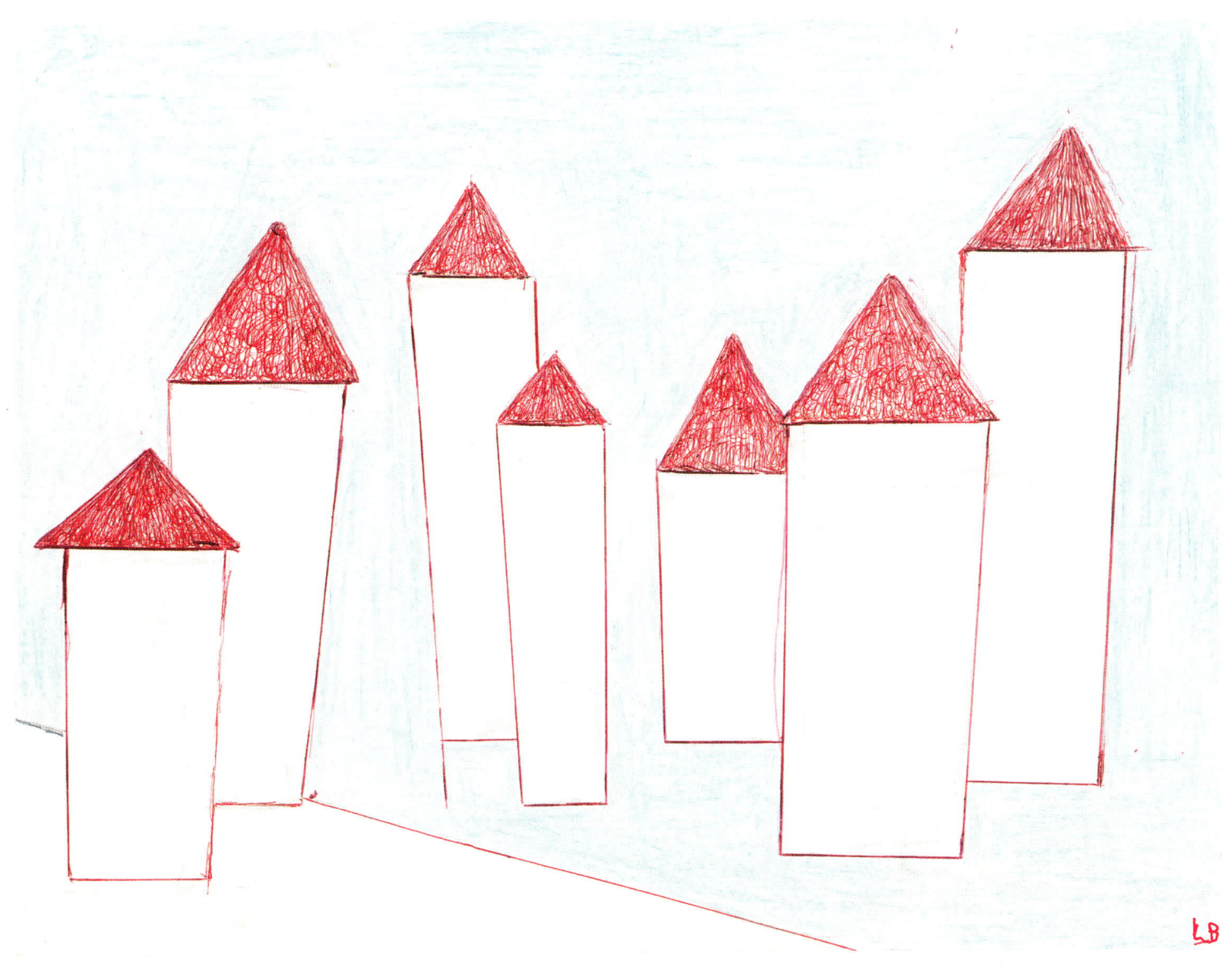

Off Balance, 1998
Rote Tinte, blauer Pastellstift und Kohle auf Papier/
Red Ink, Blue Crayon and Charcoal on Paper, 23 x 30 cm

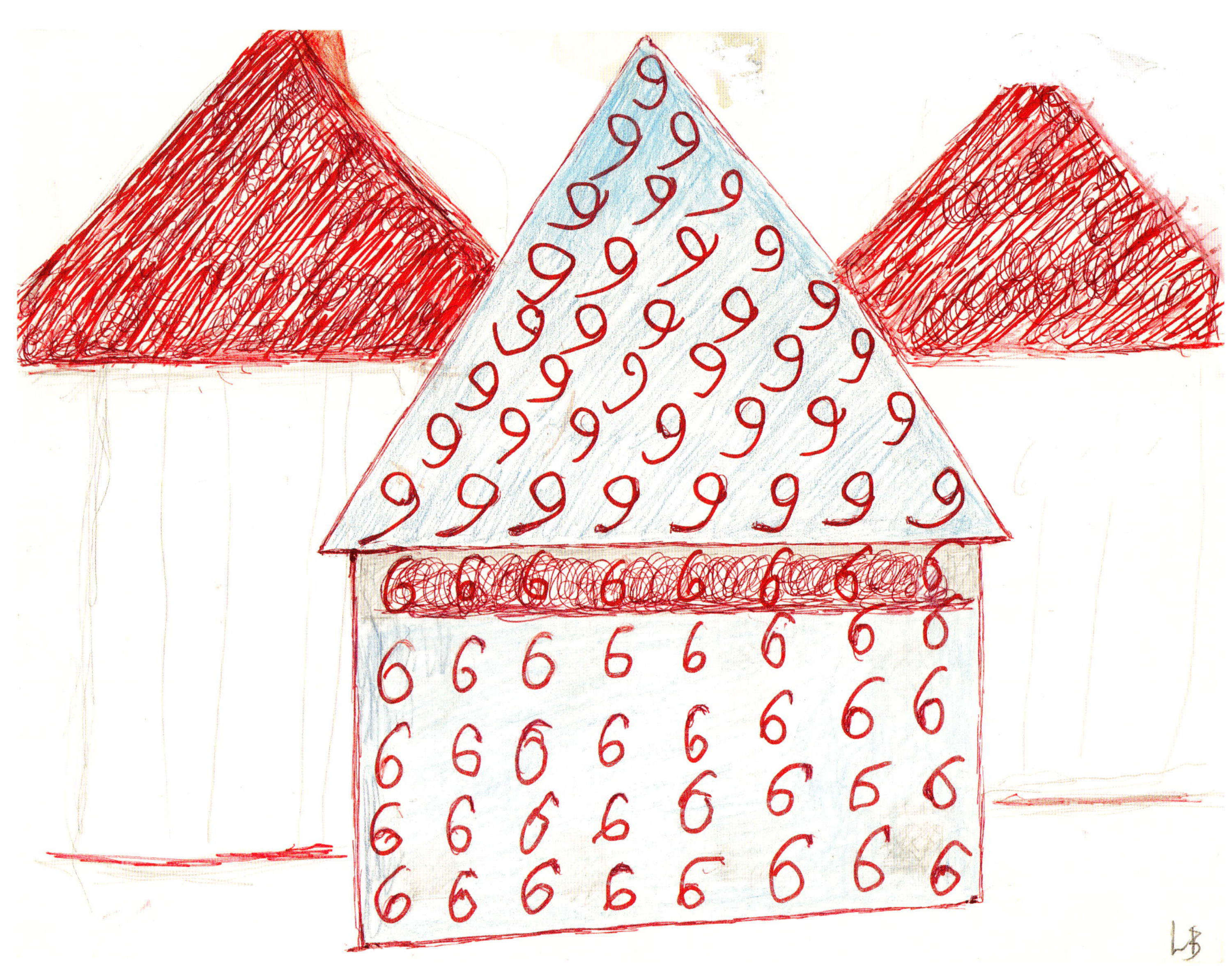

Ohne Titel/Untitled, 1997
Rote Tinte, blauer Pastellstift, weisse Gouache und Bleistift auf Papier/
Red Ink, Blue Crayon, White Gouache and Pencil on Paper, 23 x 30 cm

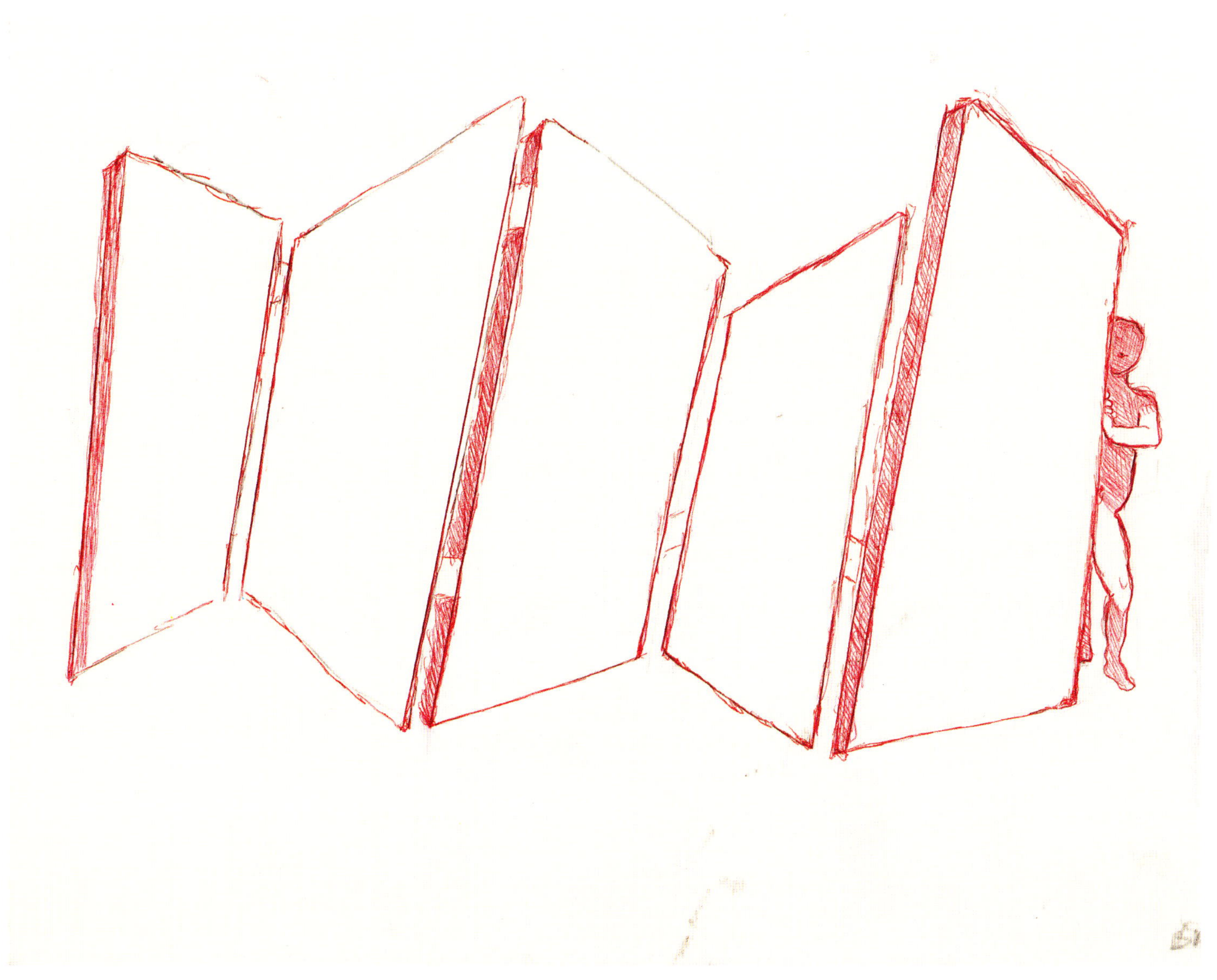

Ohne Titel/Untitled, 1997
Rote Tinte und Bleistift auf Papier/
Red Ink and Pencil on Paper, 23 x 30 cm

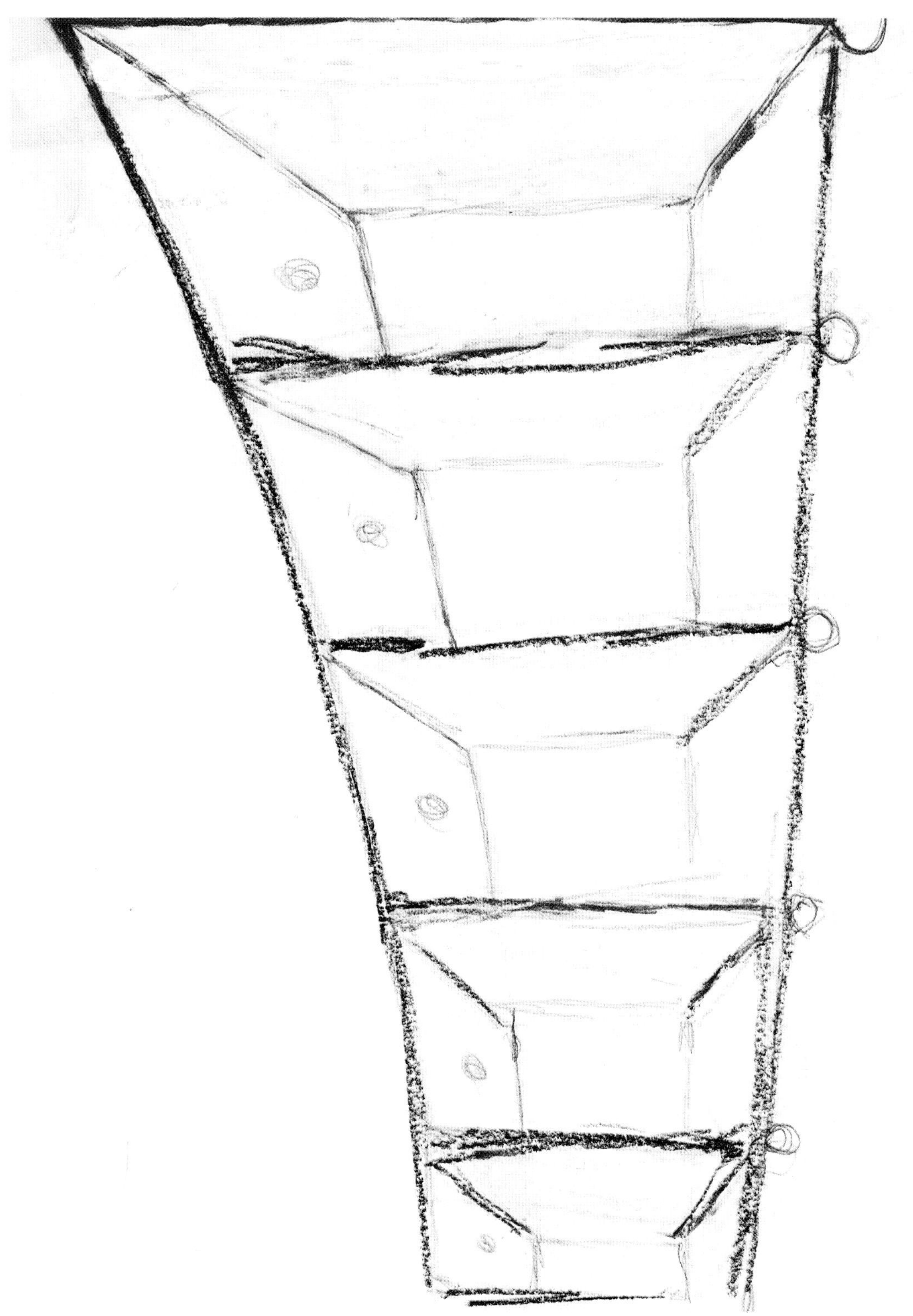

Ohne Titel/Untitled, 1997
Bleistift, Pastellstift und Gouache auf Papier/
Pencil, Crayon and Gouache on Paper, 30 x 23 cm

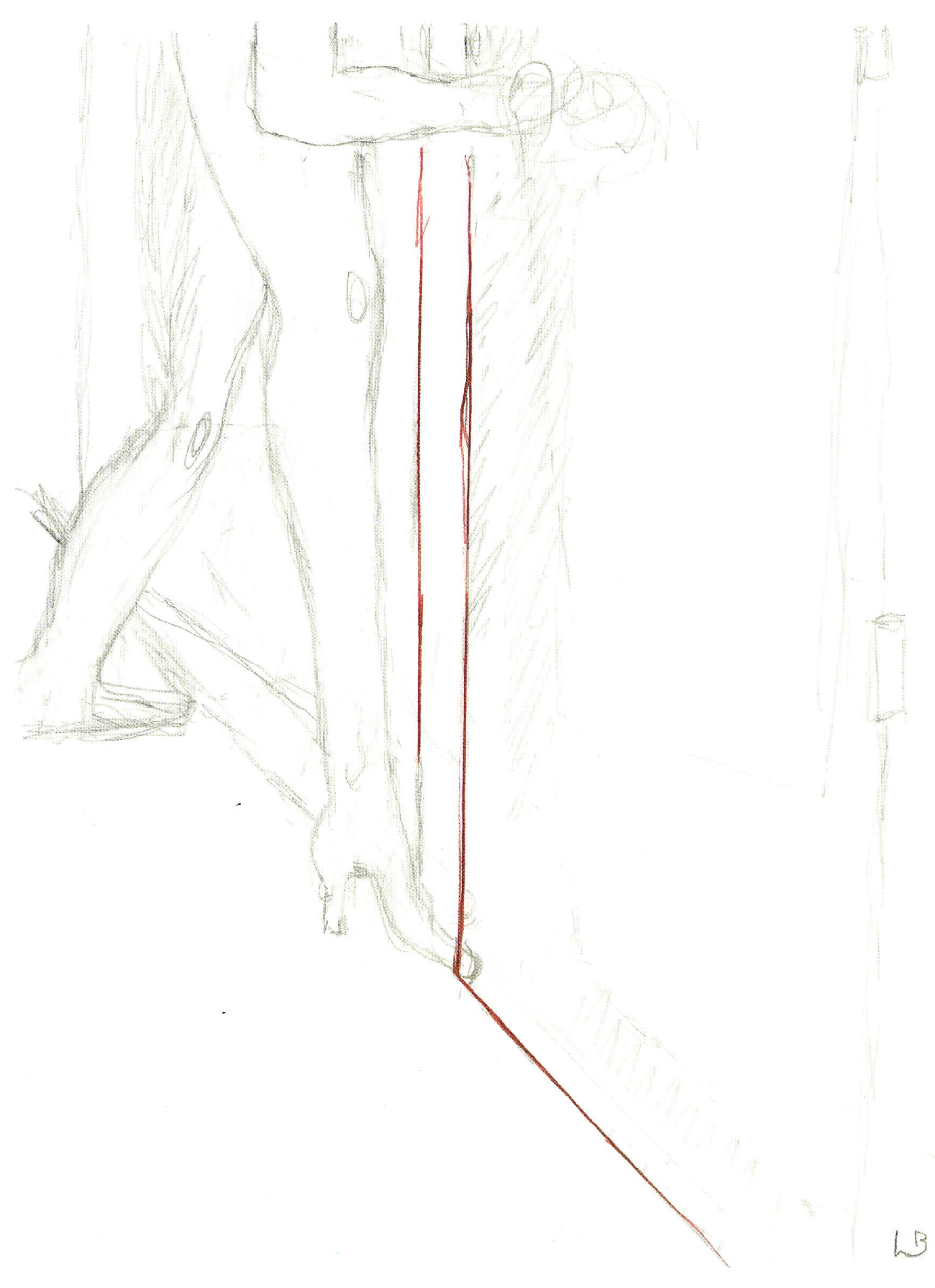

Ohne Titel/Untitled, 1998
Bleistift und rote Tinte auf Papier/
Pencil and Red Ink on Paper, 23 x 30 cm

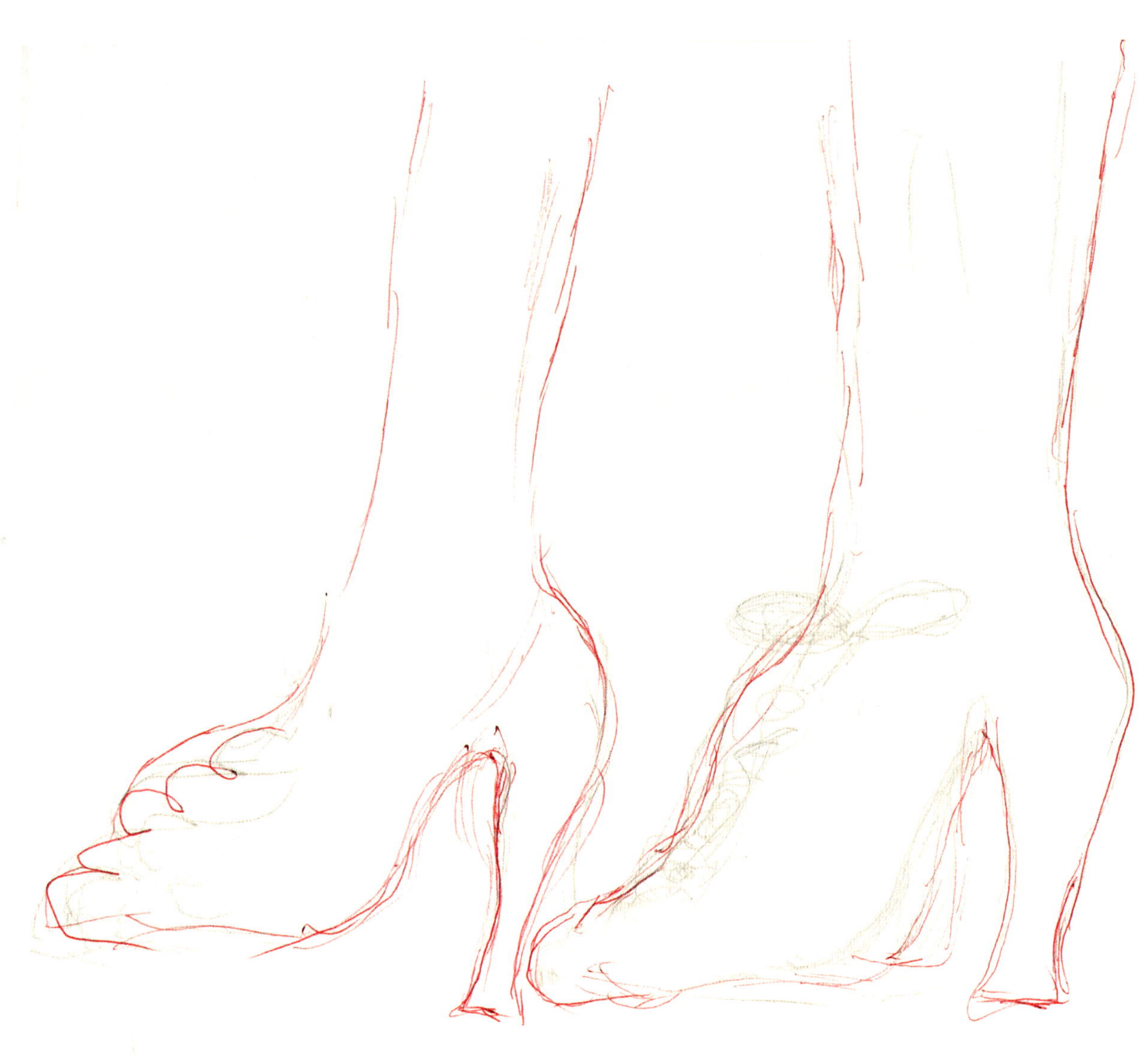

Ohne Titel/Untitled, 1997
Rote Tinte und Bleistift auf Papier/
Red Ink and Pencil on Paper, 23 x 30 cm

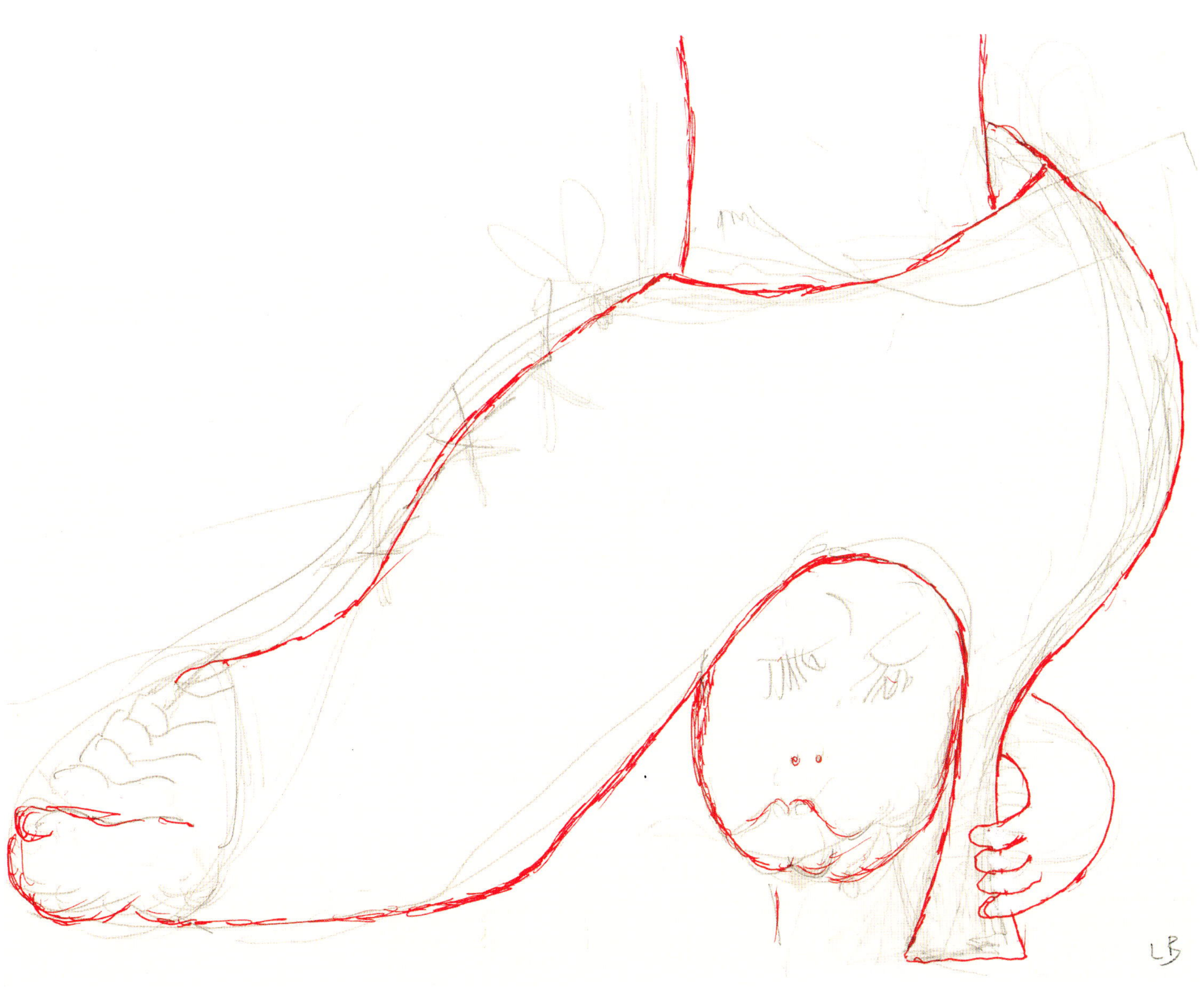

Ohne Titel/Untitled, 1998
Rote Tinte und Bleistift auf Papier/
Red Ink and Pencil on Paper, 23 x 30 cm

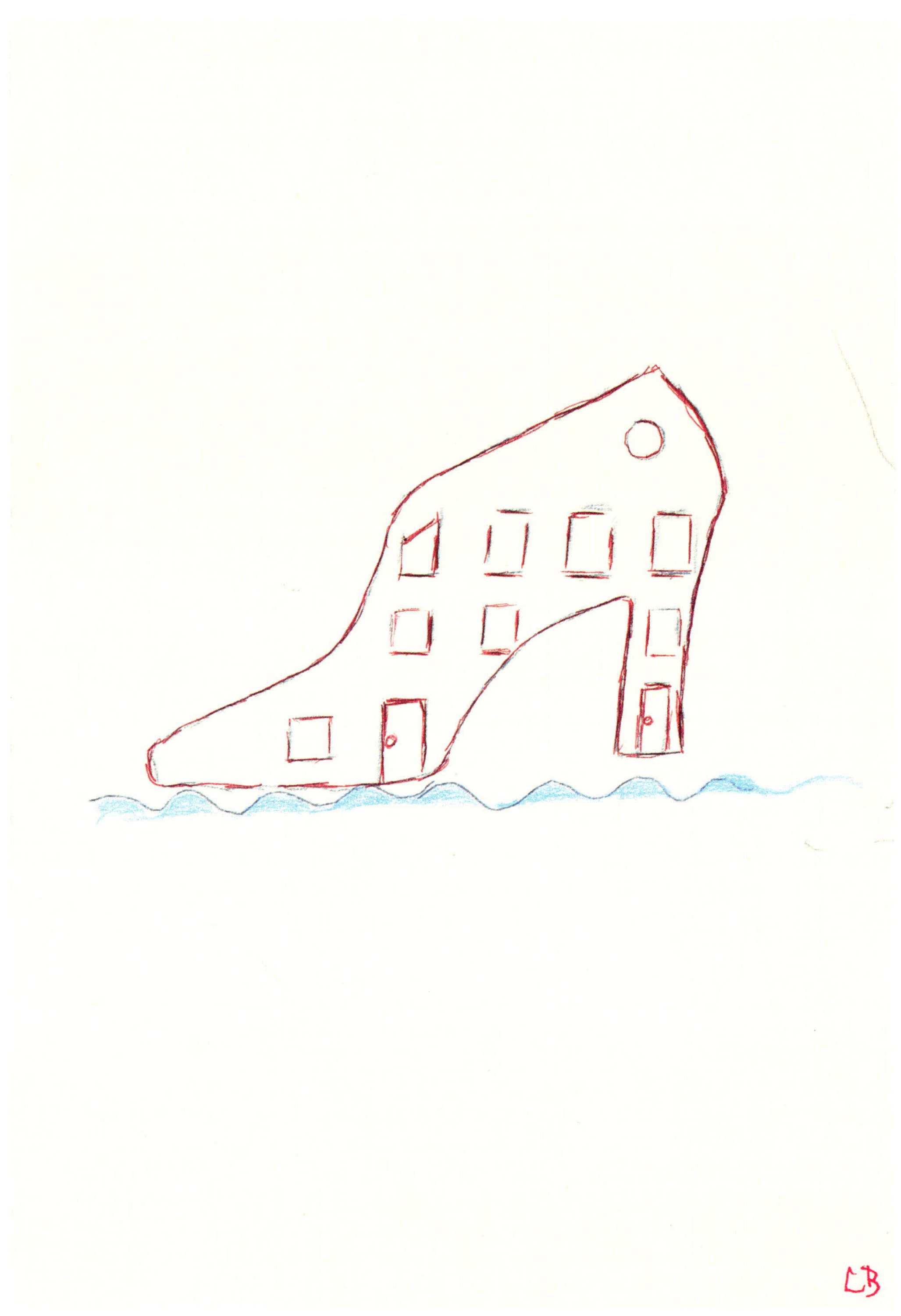

Ohne Titel/Untitled, 1996
Rote und blaue Tinte und blauer Pastellstift auf Papier/
Red and Blue Ink and Blue Crayon on Paper, 30 x 21 cm

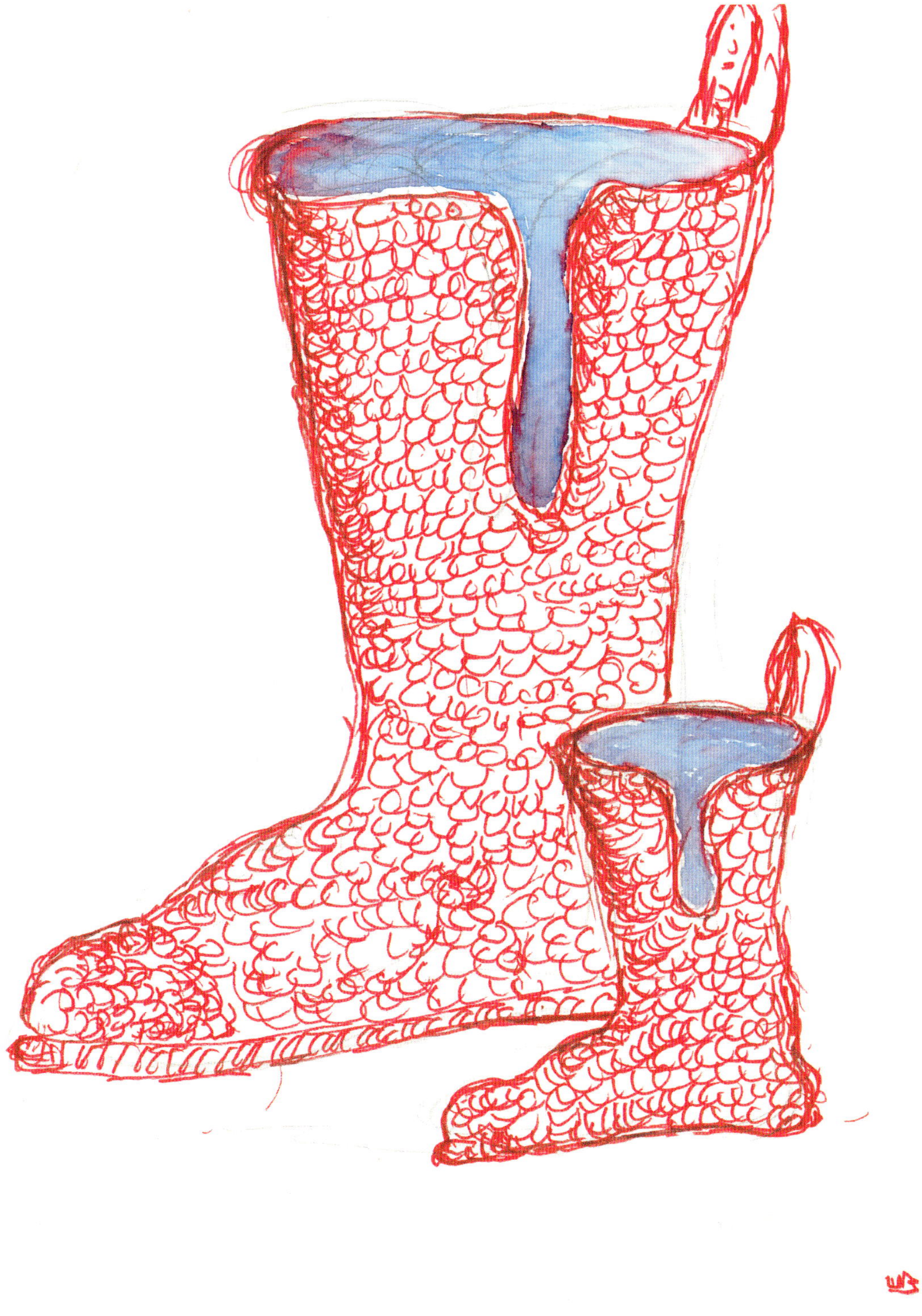

Ohne Titel/Untitled, 1997
Rote und blaue Tinte und Bleistift auf Papier/
Red and Blue Ink and Pencil on Paper, 30 x 23 cm

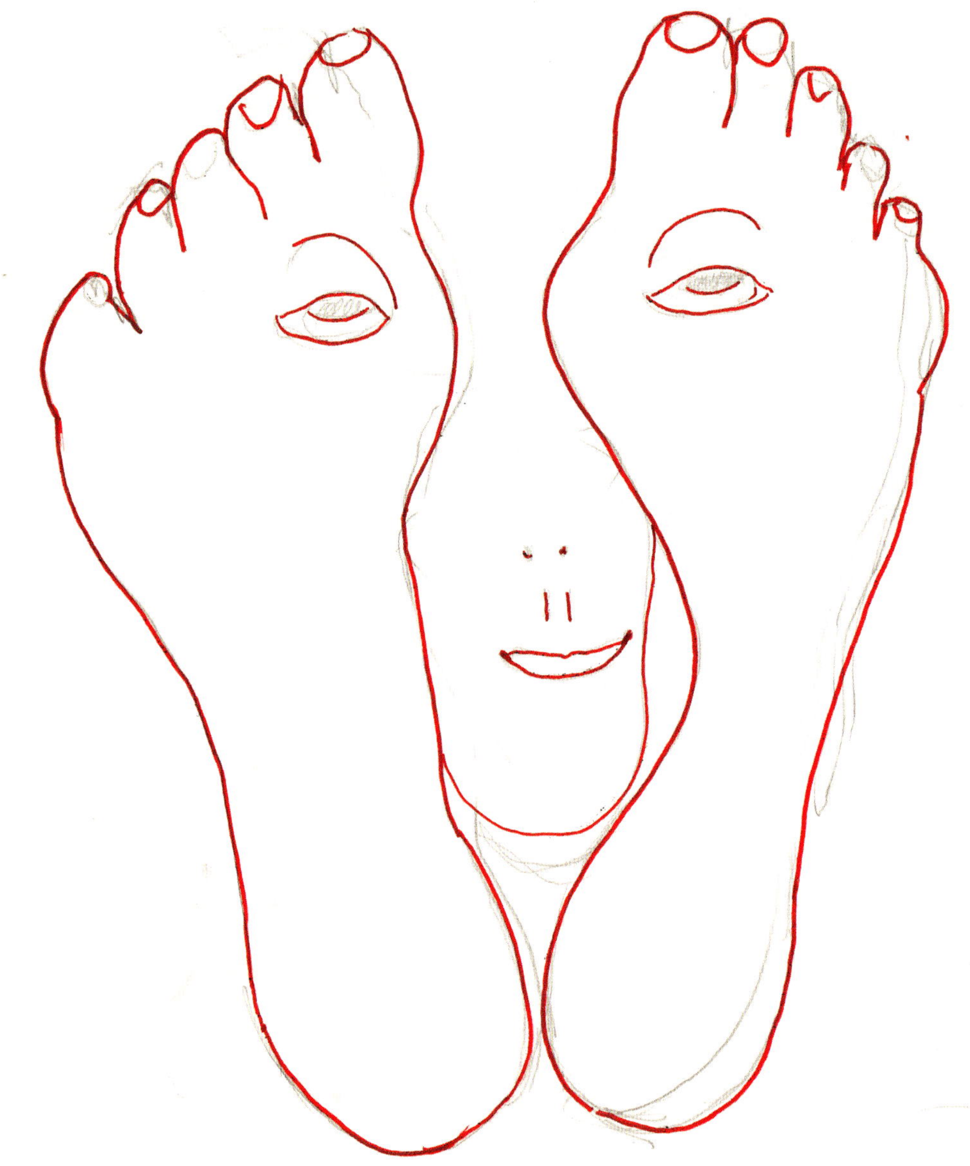

Ohne Titel/Untitled, 1996
Rote Tinte und Bleistift auf Papier/
Red Ink and Pencil on Paper, 30 x 22 cm

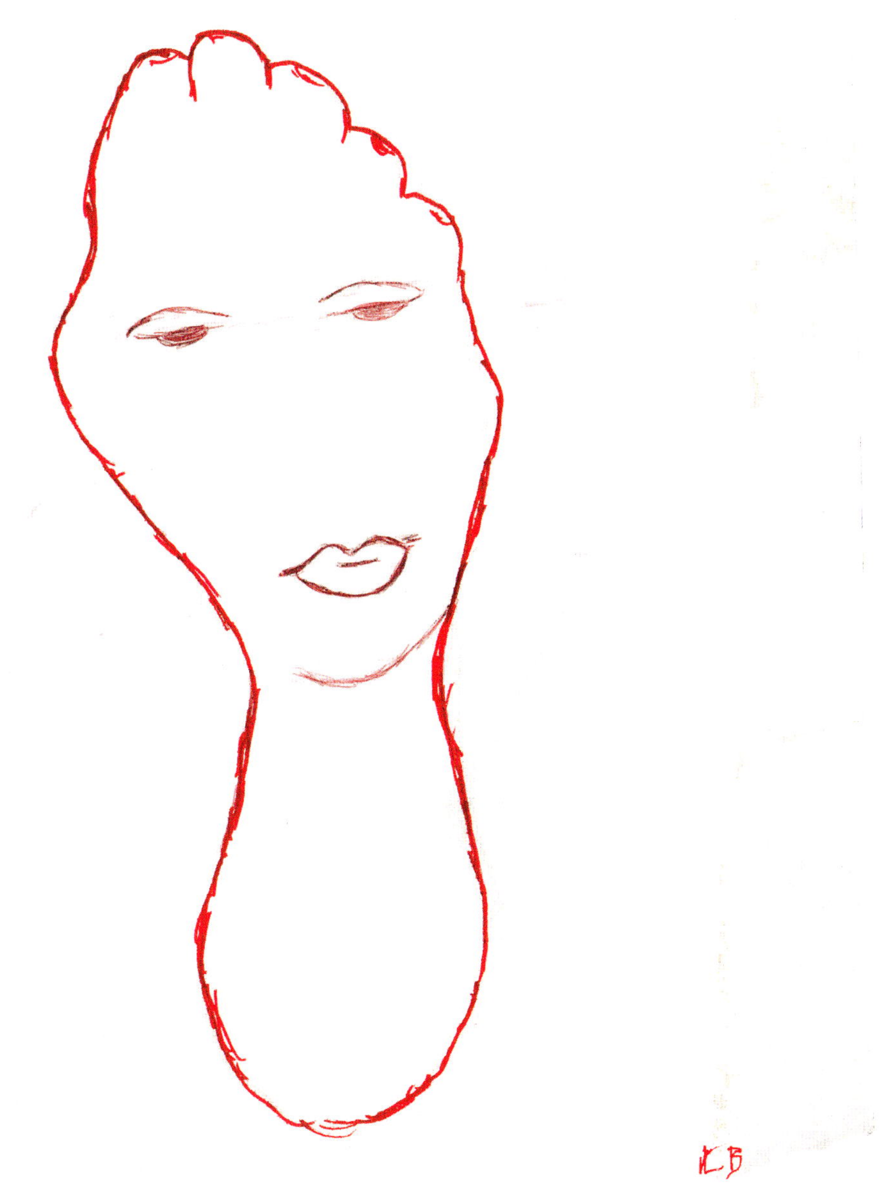

Ohne Titel/Untitled, 1996
Rote Tinte auf Papier/
Red Ink on Paper, 27 x 22 cm

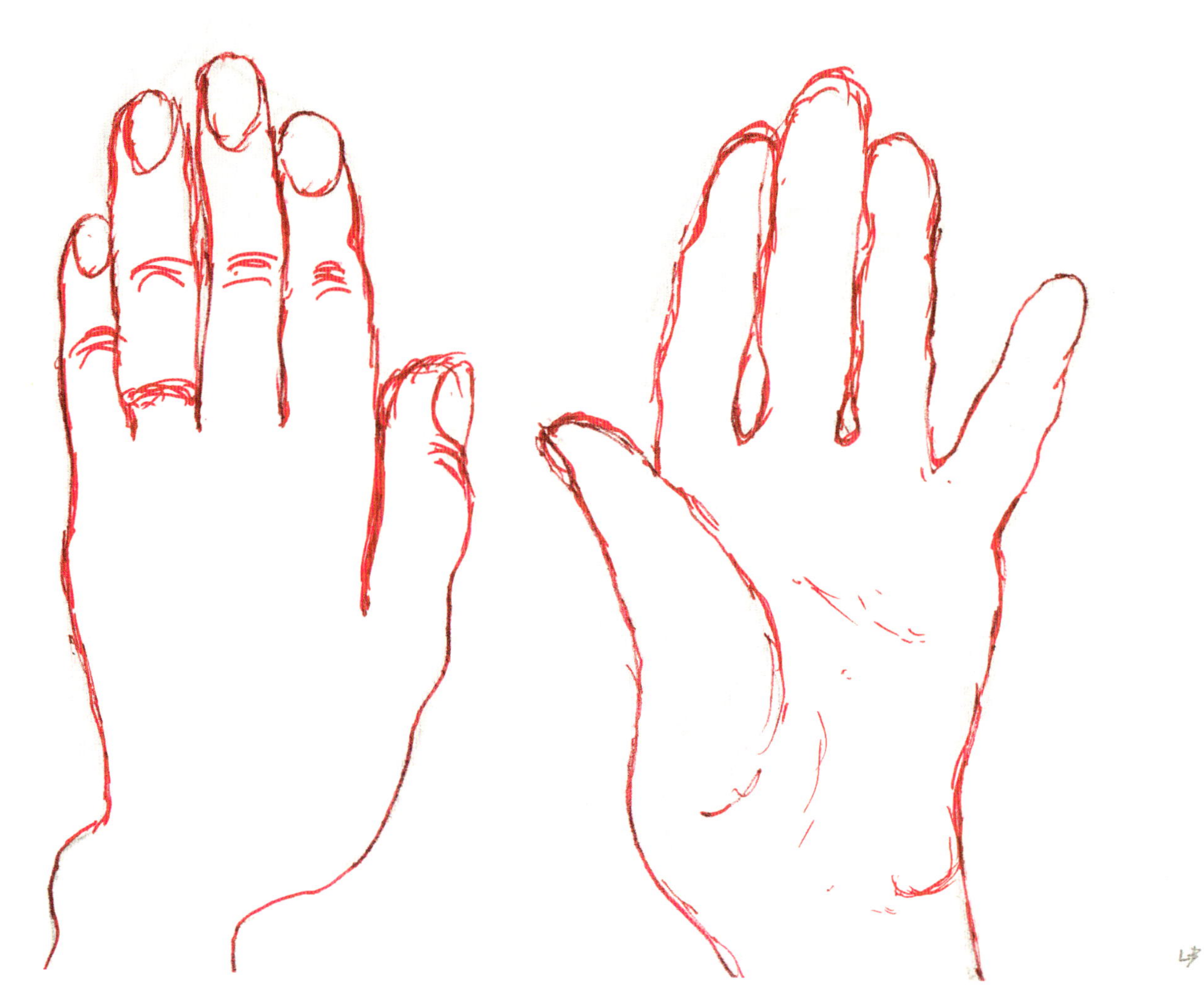

Ohne Titel/Untitled, 1996
Rote Tinte und Kohle auf Papier/
Red Ink and Charcoal on Paper, 23 x 30 cm

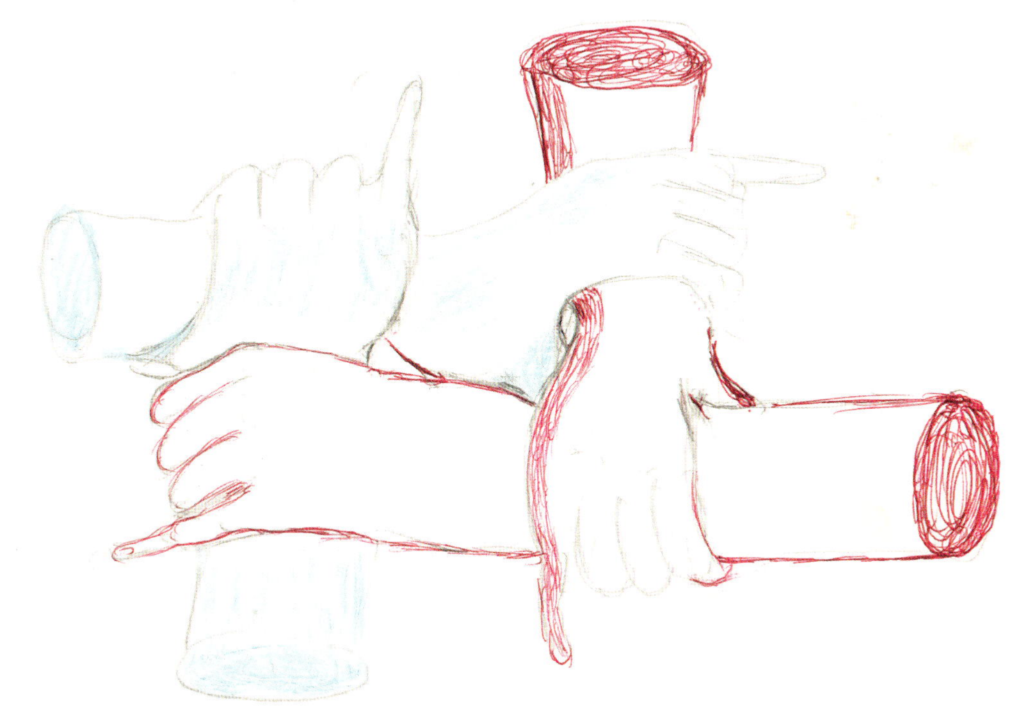

The Pinky, 1998
Rote Tinte, blauer Pastellstift und Bleistift auf Papier/
Red Ink, Blue Crayon and Pencil on Paper, 22 x 28 cm

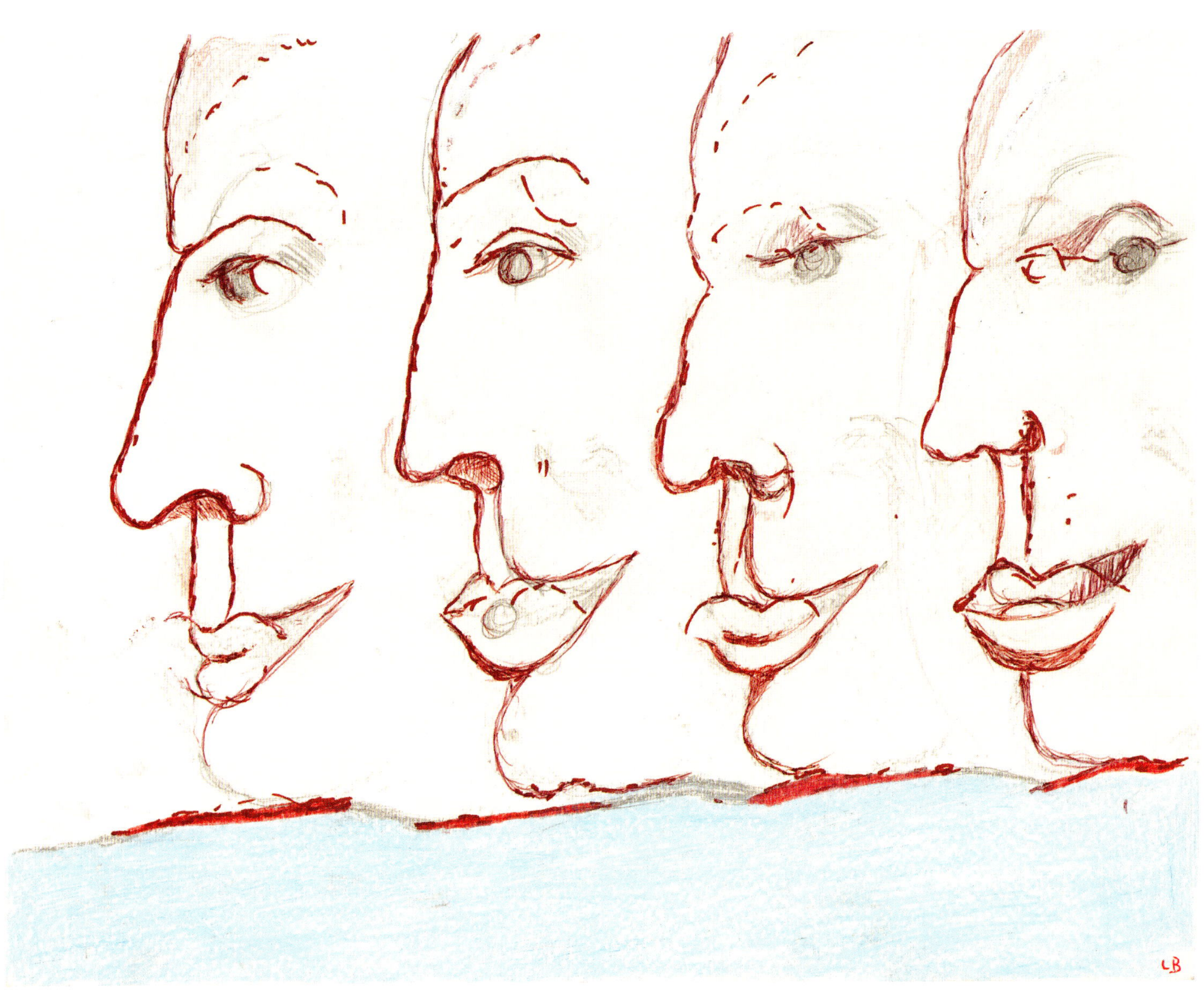

Ohne Titel/Untitled, 1997 (?)
Rote Tinte, blauer Pastellstift, weiße Gouache und Bleistift auf Papier/
Red Ink, Blue Crayon, White Gouache and Pencil on Paper, 23 x 30 cm

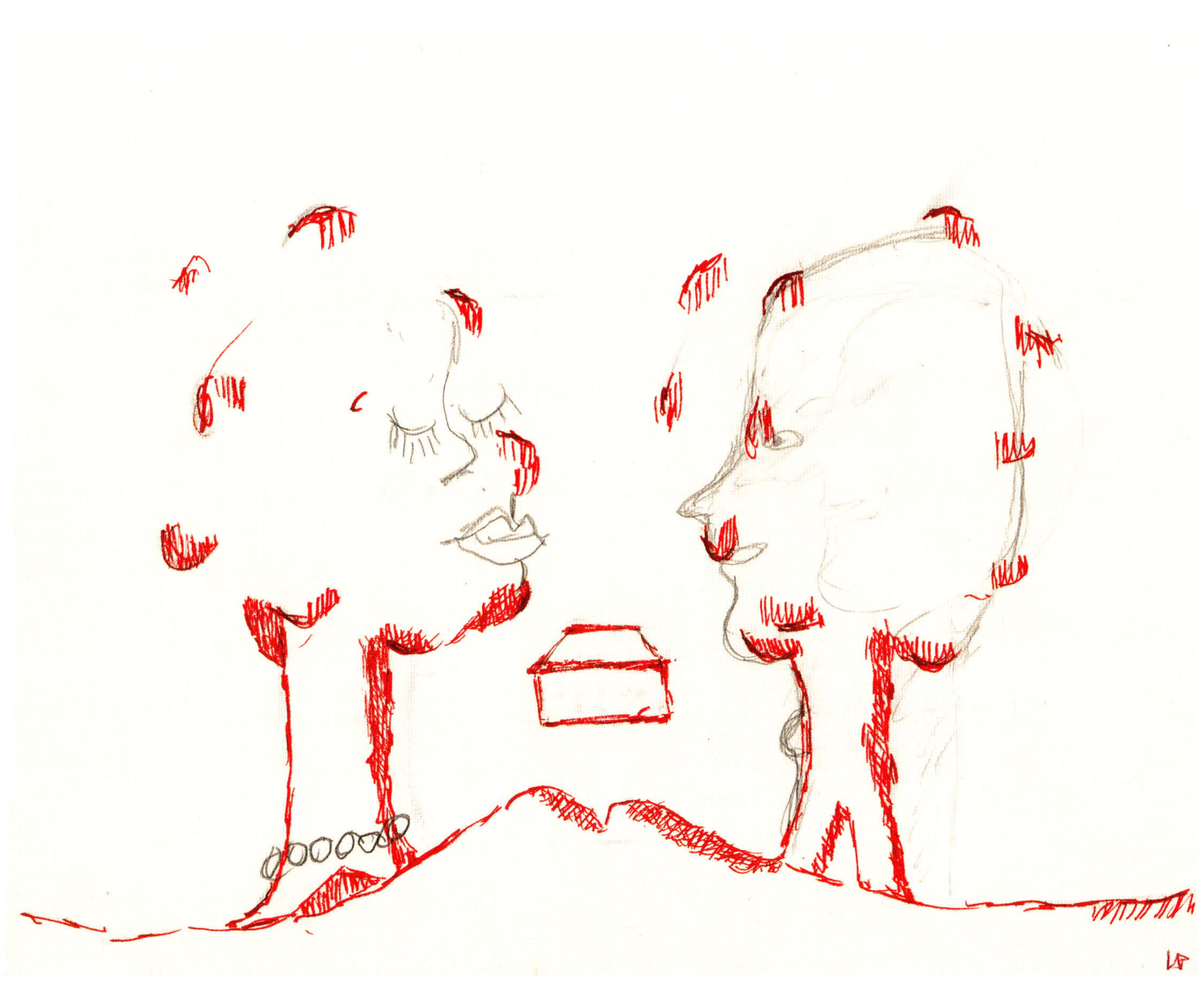

Confrontation, 1998
Rote Tinte und Bleistift auf Papier/
Red Ink and Pencil on Paper, 23 x 30 cm

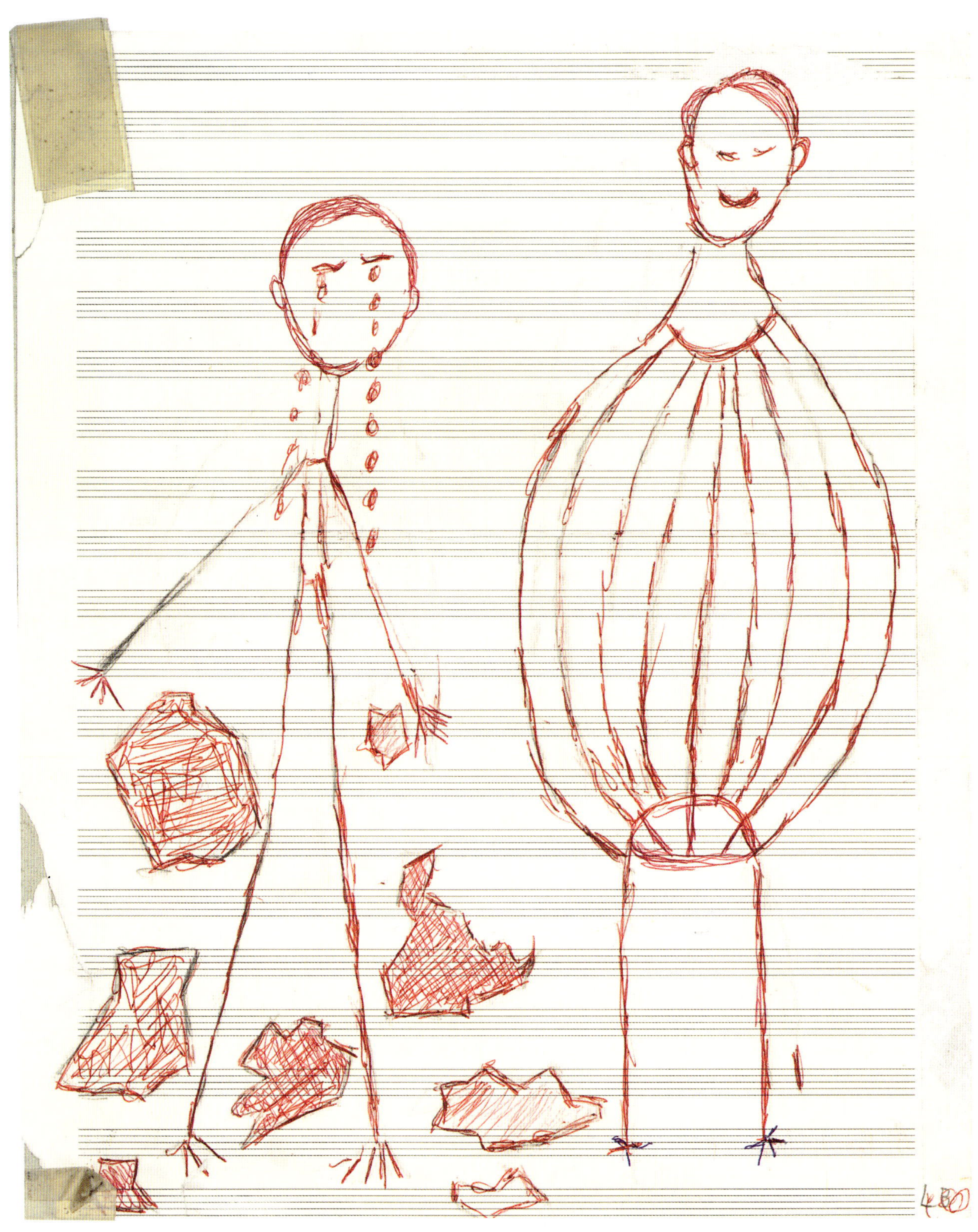

Le Pot de Terre et le Pot de Fer, 1998
Rote Tinte, Bleistift und Abdeckband auf Notenpapier/
Red Ink, Pencil and Masking Tape on Music Paper, 32 x 27 cm

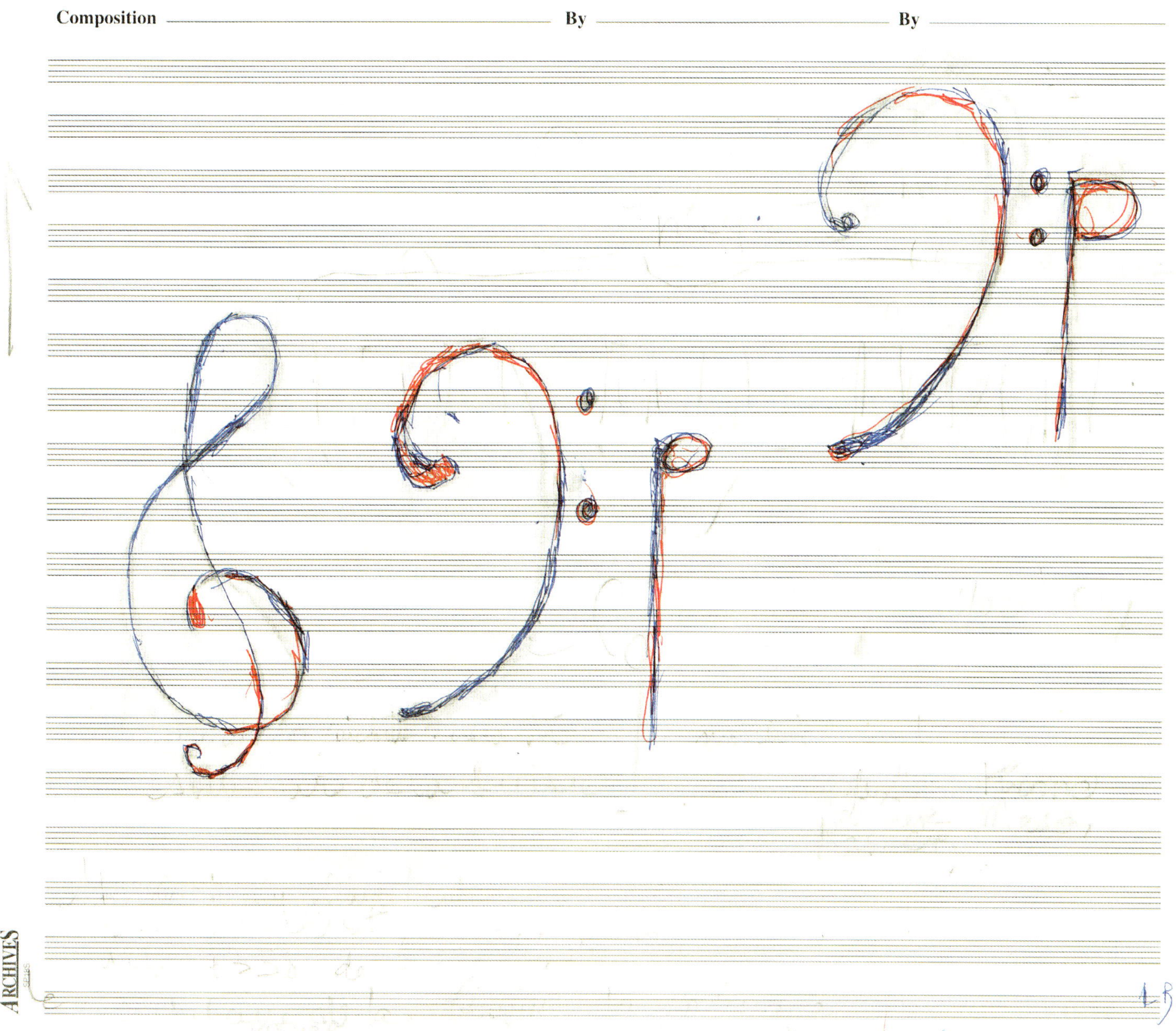

Ohne Titel/Untitled, 1998
Rote und blaue Tinte und Bleistift auf Notenpapier/
Red and Blue Ink and Pencil on Music Paper, 28 x 32 cm

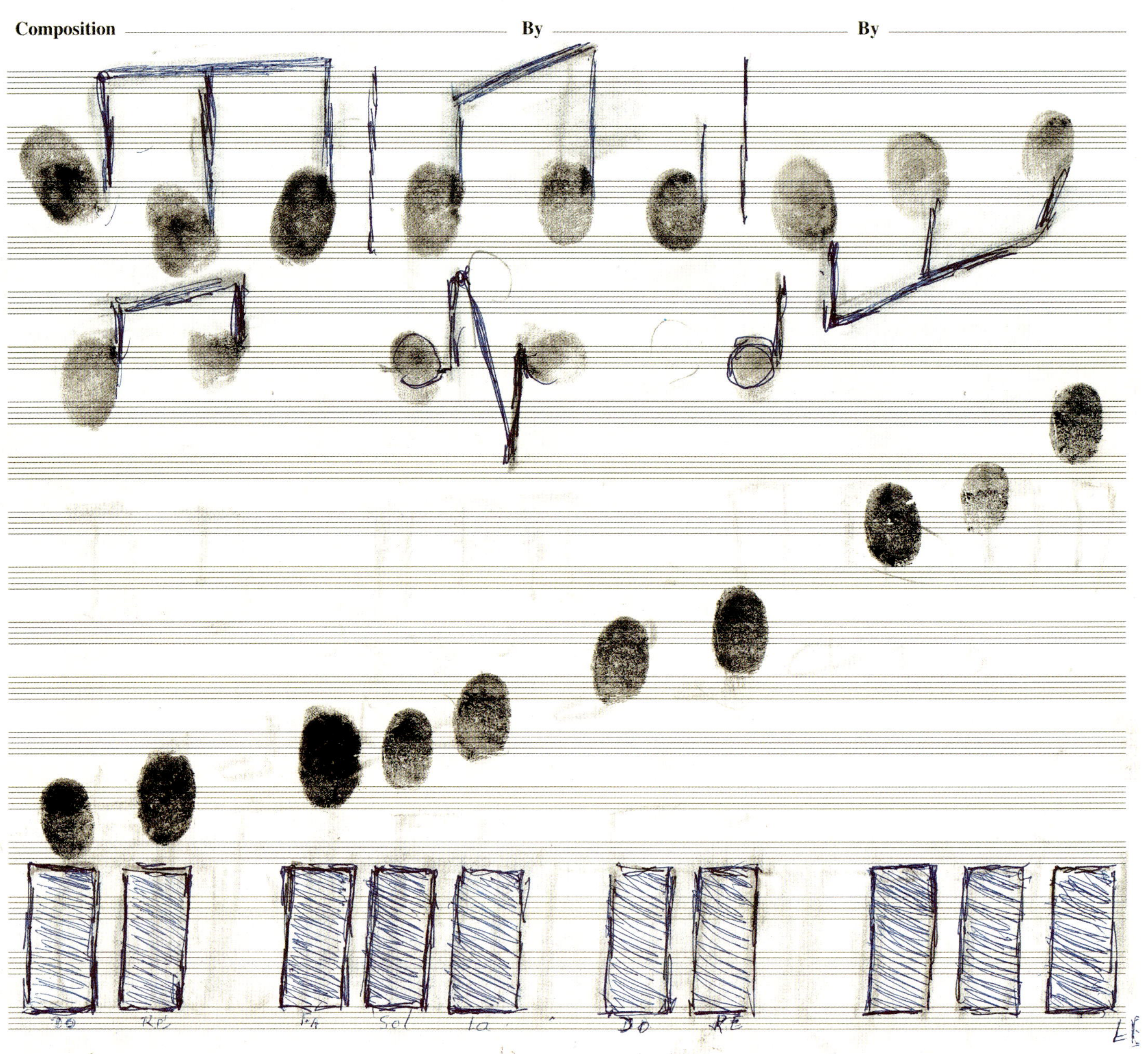

Ohne Titel/Untitled, 1998
Blaue Tinte und Kohle auf Notenpapier/
Blue Ink and Charcoal on Music Paper, 28 x 32 cm

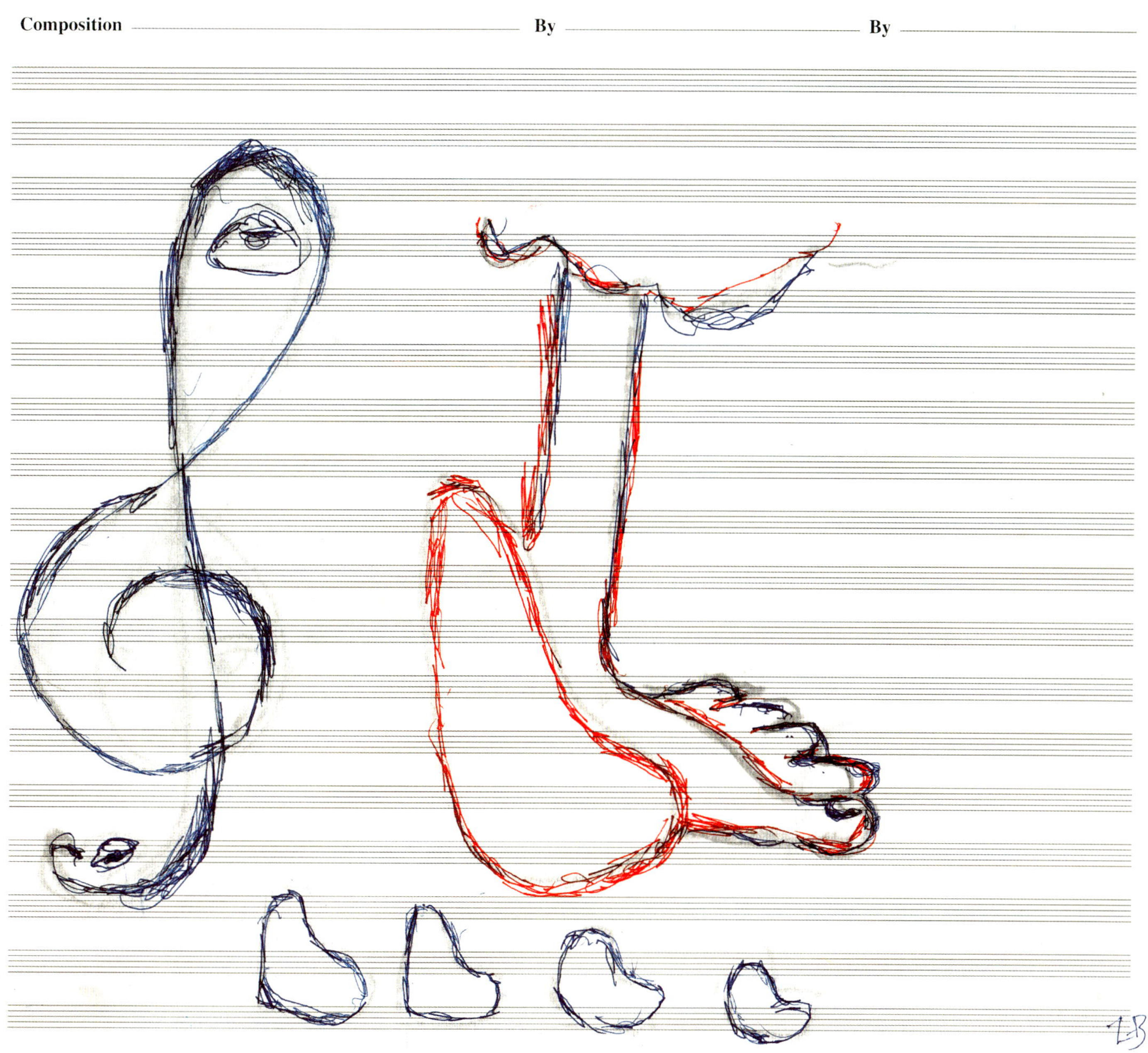

La Blessure au Pied, 1998
Rote und blaue Tinte und Kohle auf Notenpapier/
Red and Blue Ink and Charcoal on Music Paper, 28 x 32 cm

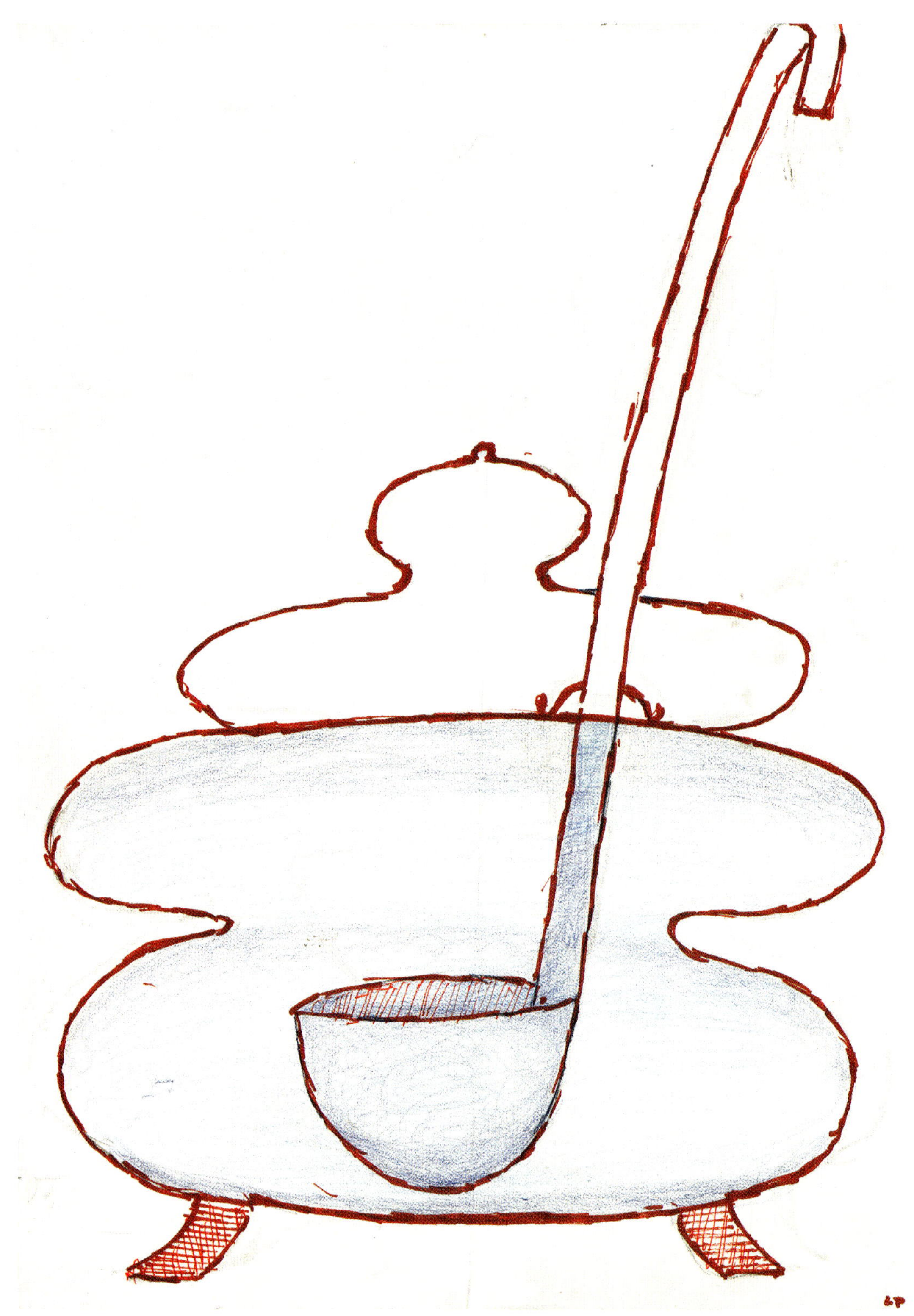

Ohne Titel/Untitled, 1997
Rote Tinte und blauer Pastellstift auf Papier/
Red Ink and Blue Crayon on Paper, 30 x 23 cm

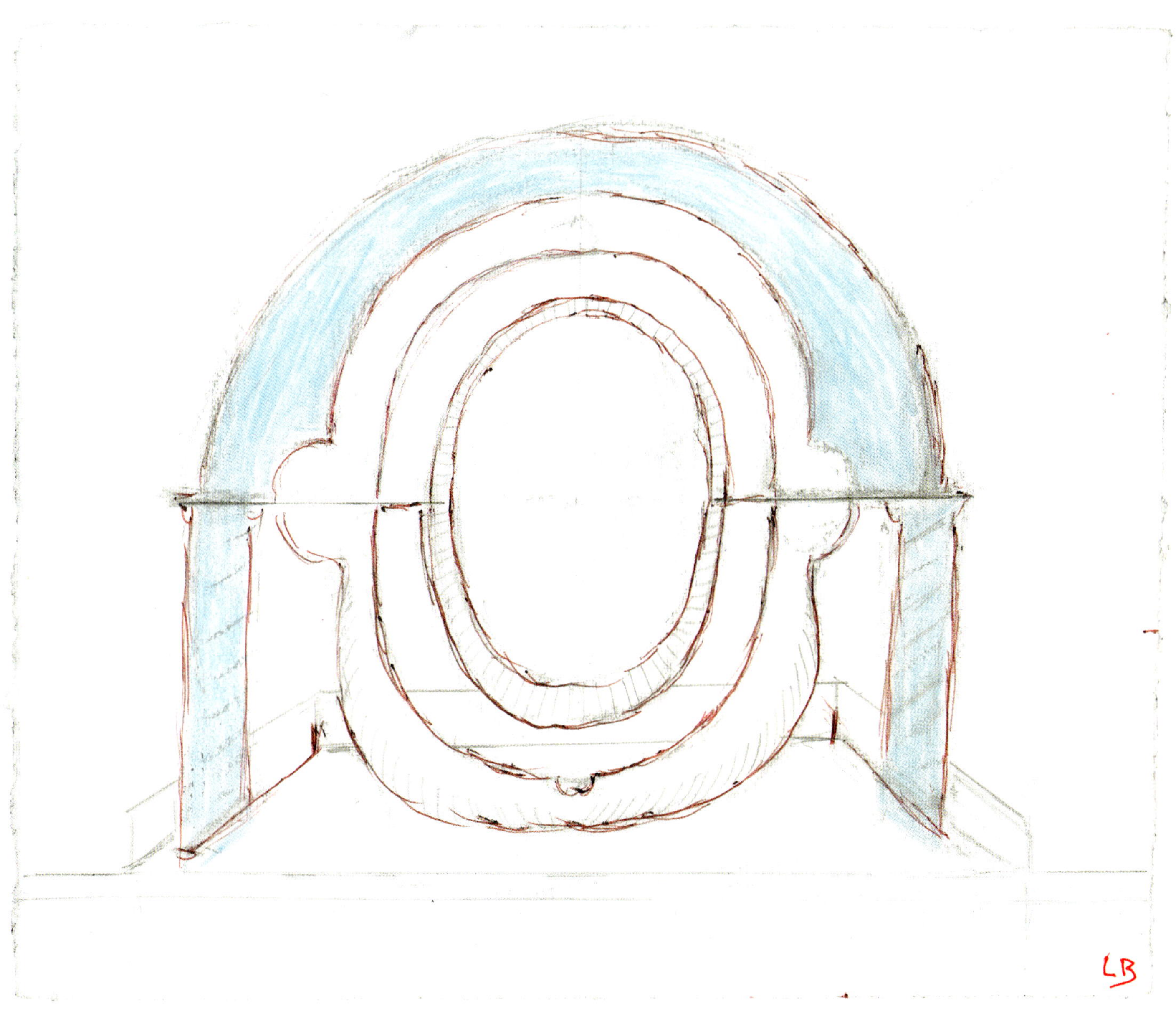

Ohne Titel/Untitled, 1998
Rote Tinte, blauer Pastellstift und Bleistift auf Papier/
Red Ink, Blue Crayon and Pencil on Paper, 23 x 28 cm

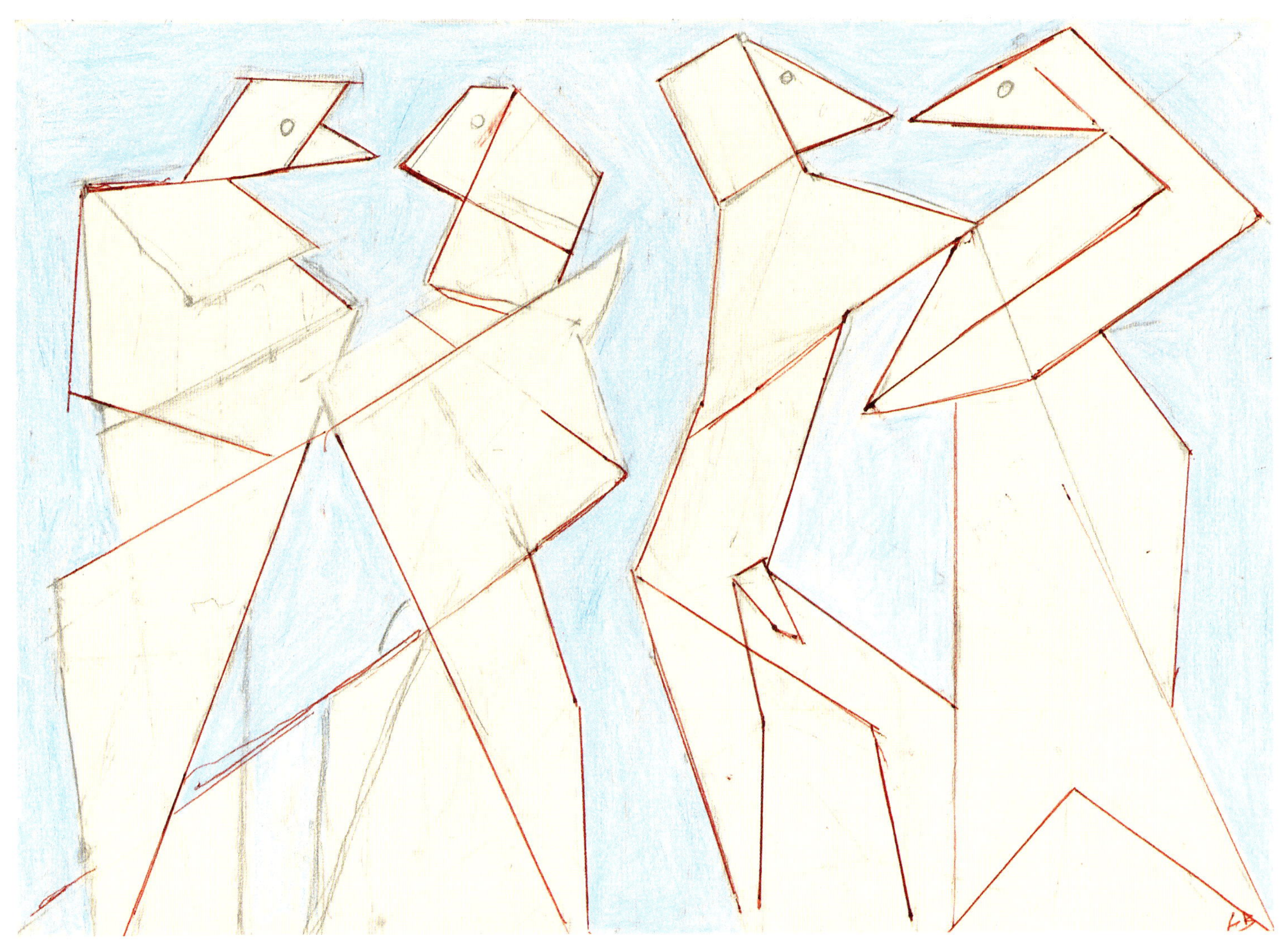

Ohne Titel/Untitled, 1997
Rote Tinte, blauer Pastellstift und Bleistift auf Papier/
Red Ink, Blue Crayon and Pencil on Paper, 21 x 30 cm

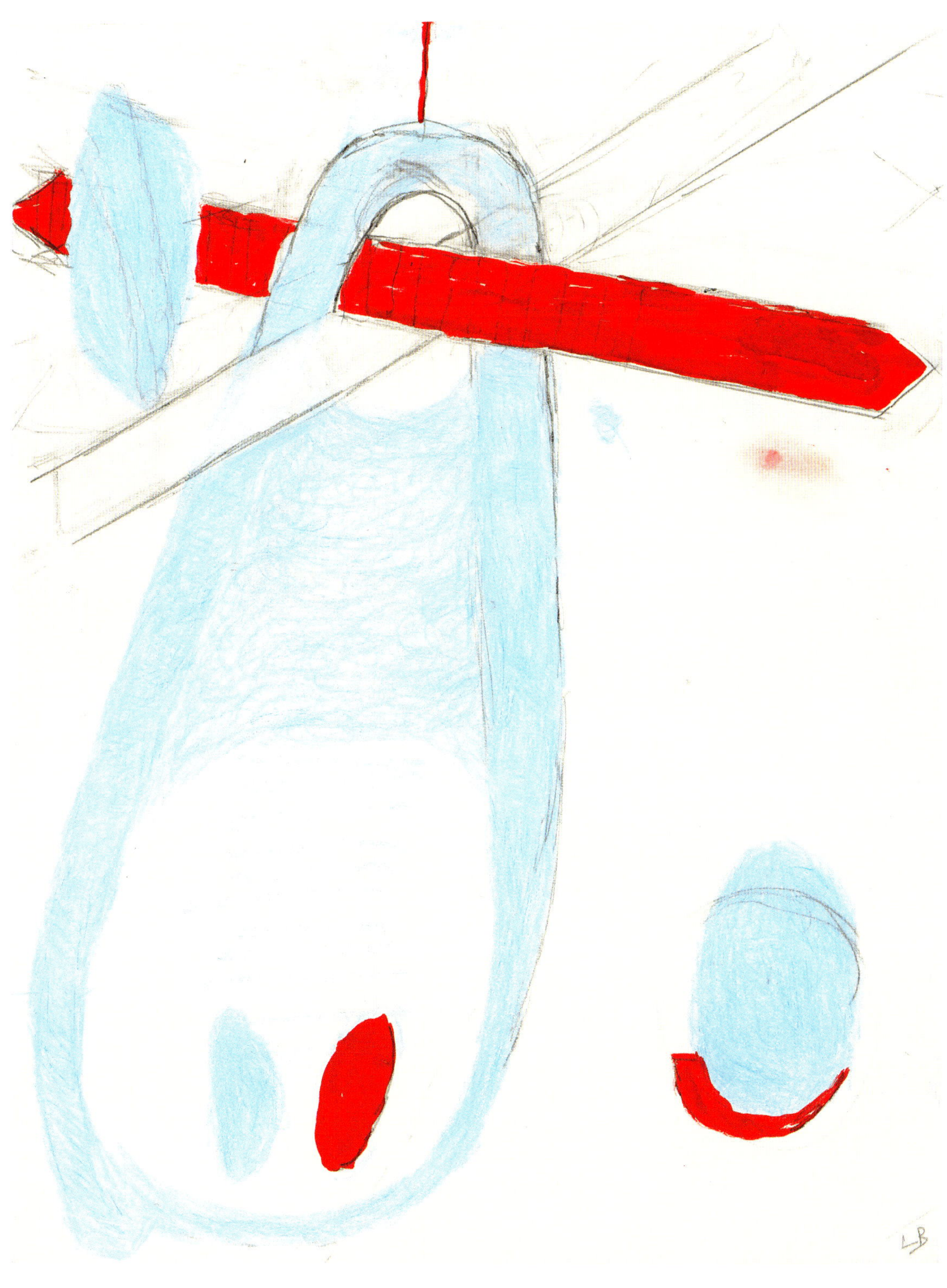

Ohne Titel/Untitled, 1997
Rote Tusche, blaue Pastellstift und Bleistift auf Papier/
Red Watercolor, Blue Crayon and Pencil on Paper, 30 x 23 cm

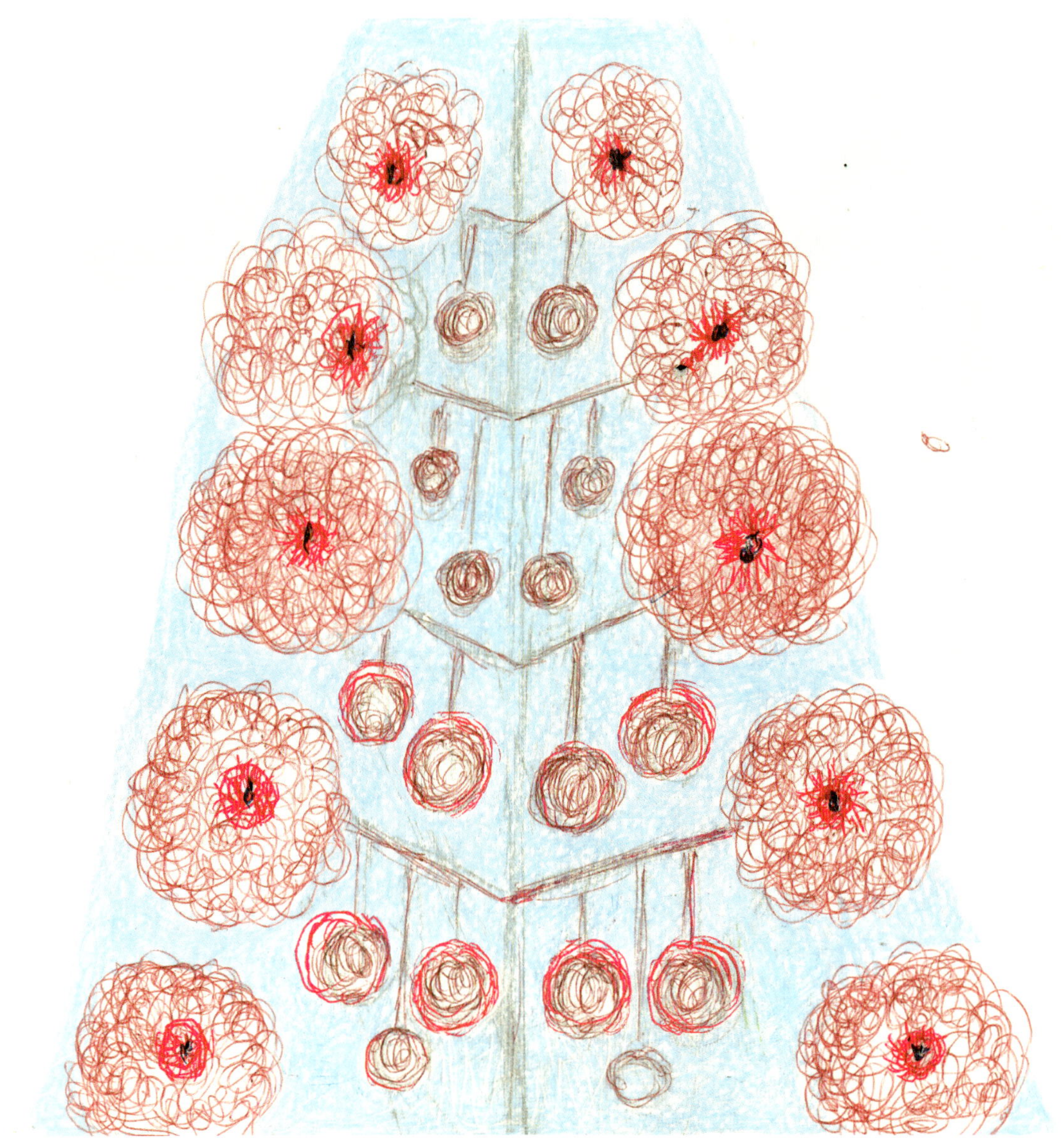

Ohne Titel/Untitled, 1997
Rote Tinte, blauer Pastellstift und Bleistift auf Papier/
Red Ink, Blue Crayon and Pencil on Paper, 23 x 30 cm

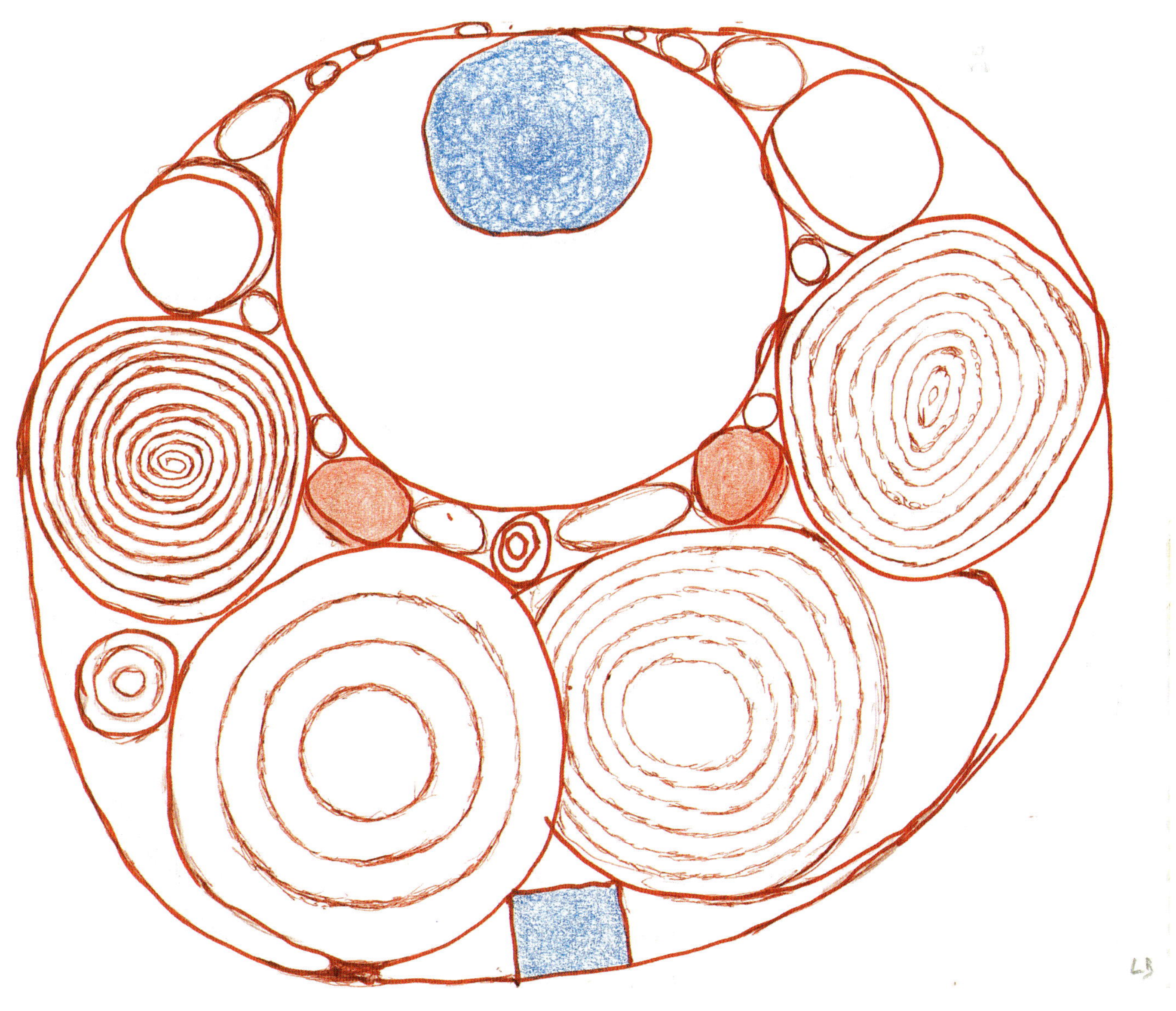

Ohne Titel/Untitled, 1997
Rote Tinte, blauer Pastellstift und Bleistift auf Papier/
Red Ink, Blue Crayon and Pencil on Paper, 23 x 30 cm

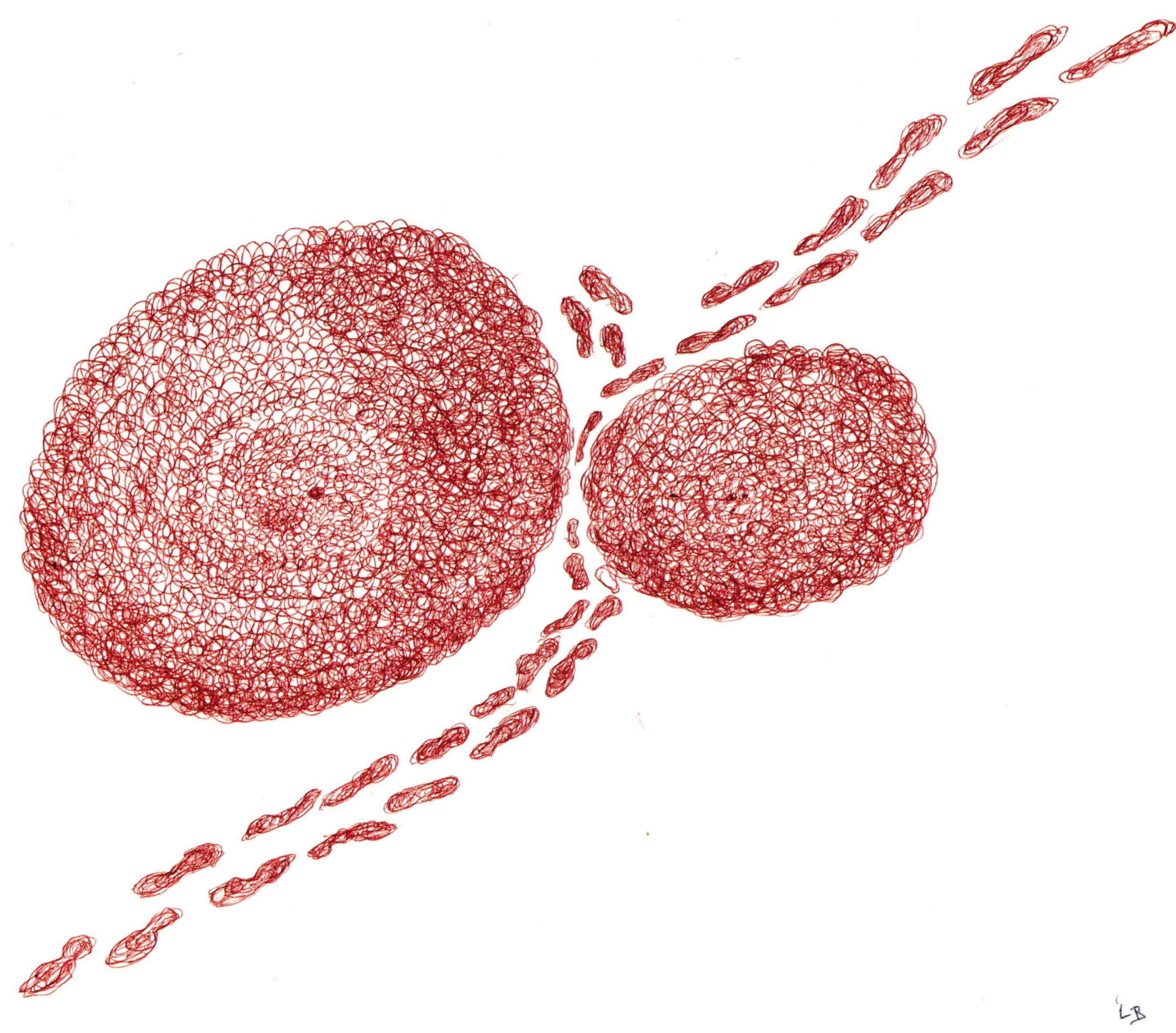

Ohne Titel/Untitled, 1998
Rote Tinte auf Papier/
Red Ink on Paper, 23 x 30 cm

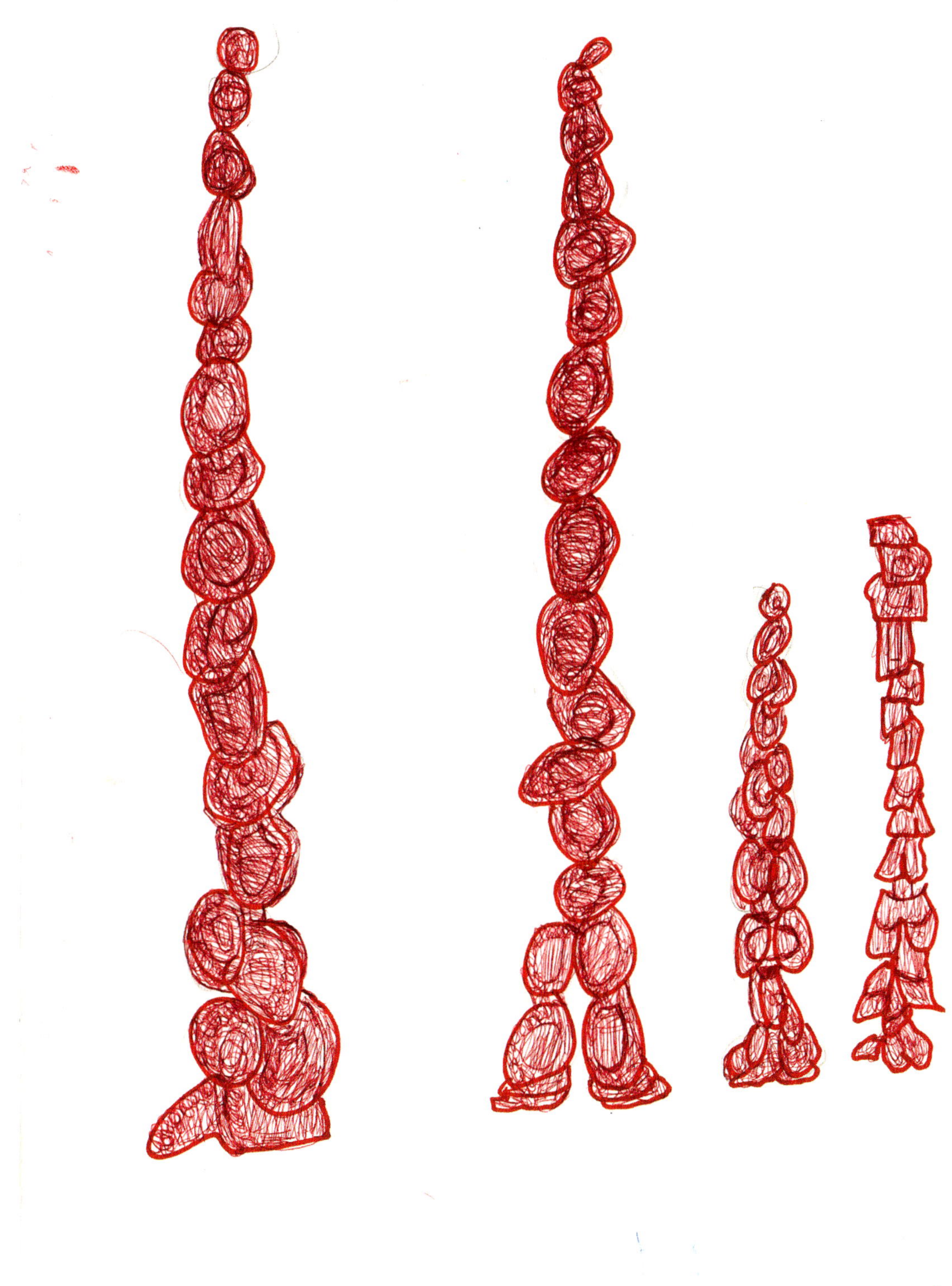

Ohne Titel/Untitled, 1997
Rote Tinte auf Papier/
Red Ink on Paper, 30 x 22 cm

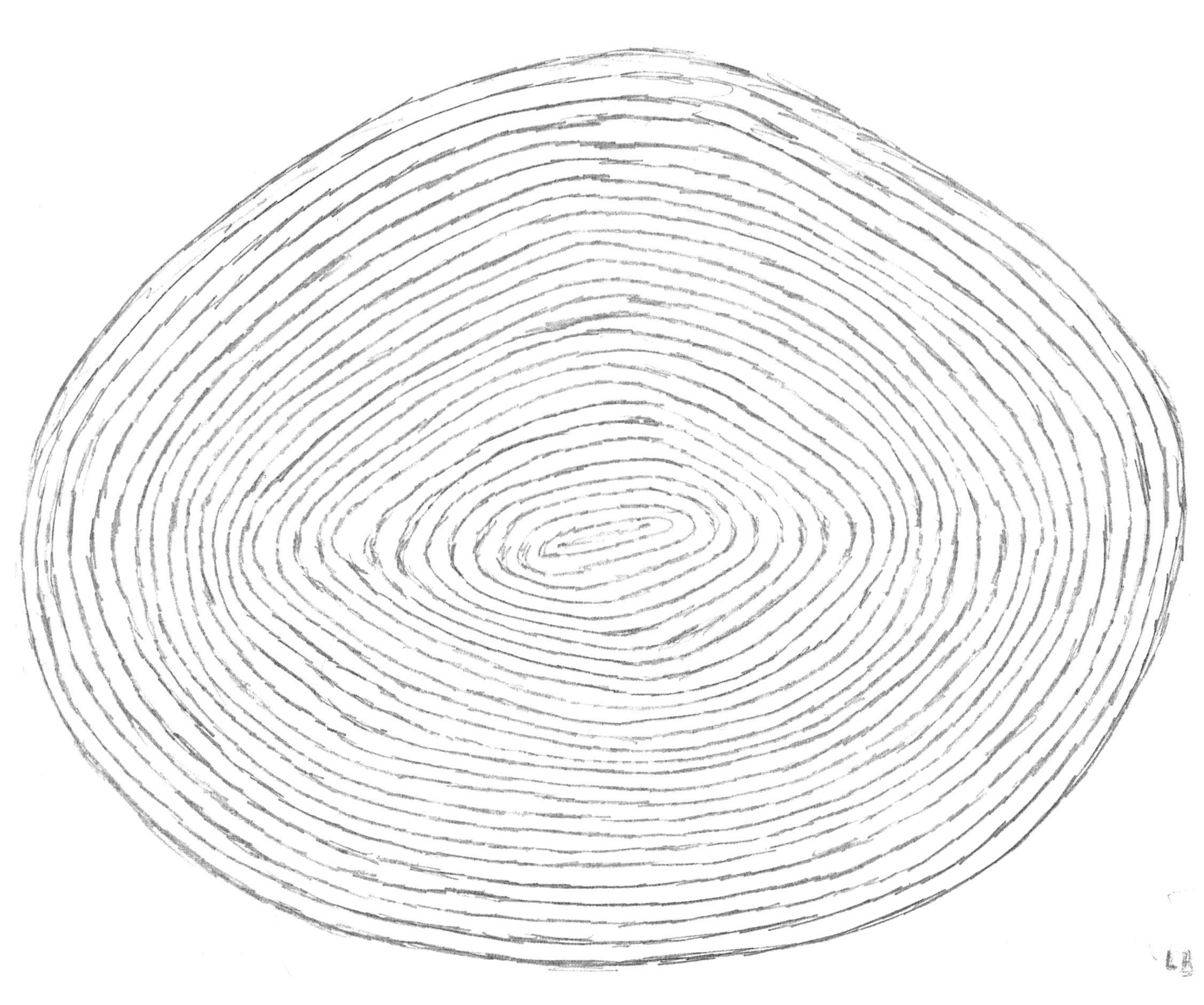

Ohne Titel/Untitled, 1998
Bleistift auf Papier/
Pencil on Paper, 23 x 30 cm

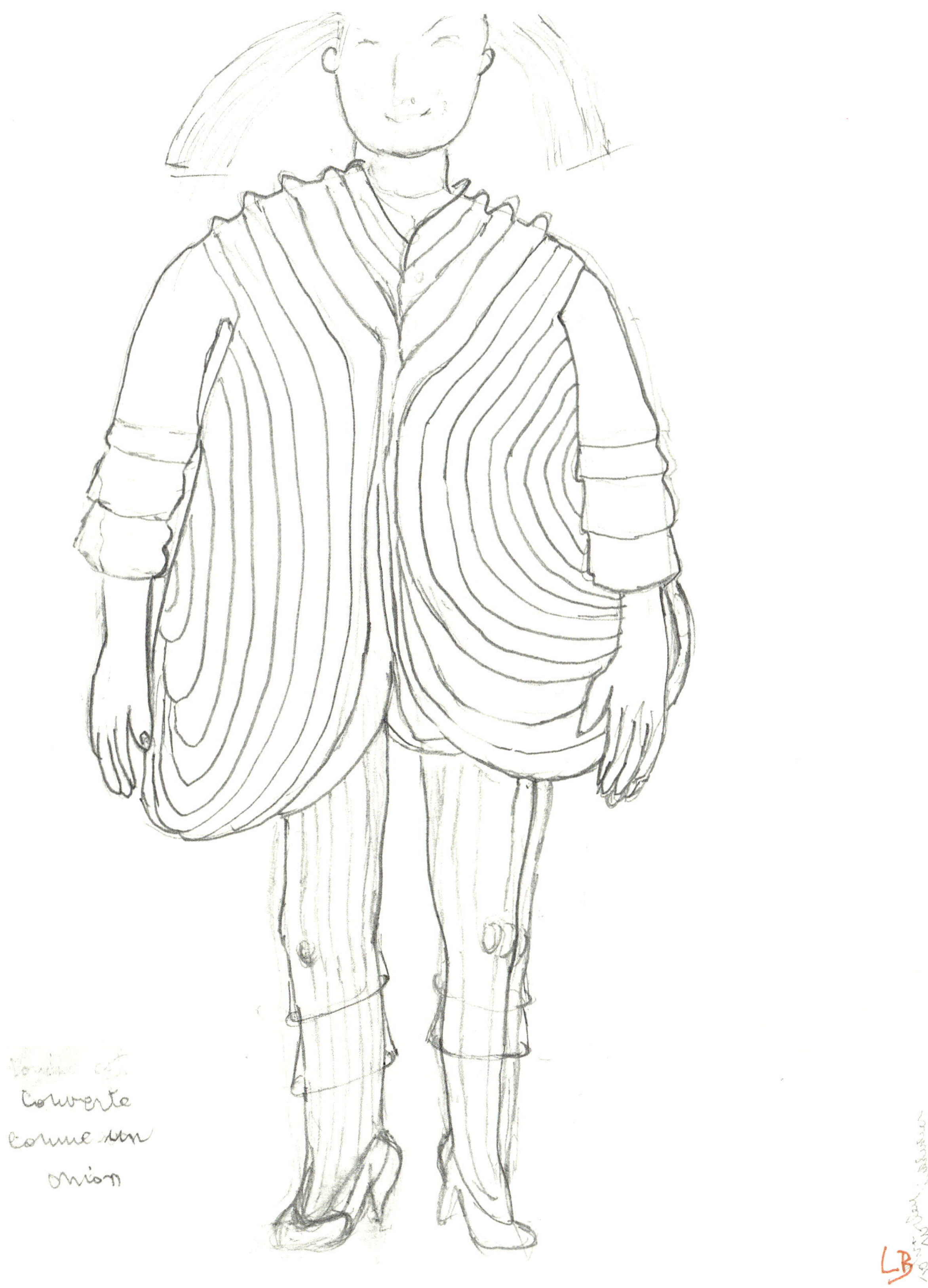

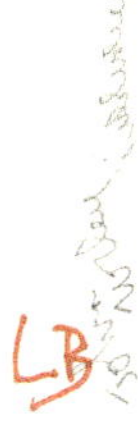

Ohne Titel/Untitled, 1998
Bleistift auf Papier/
Pencil on Paper, 30 x 23 cm

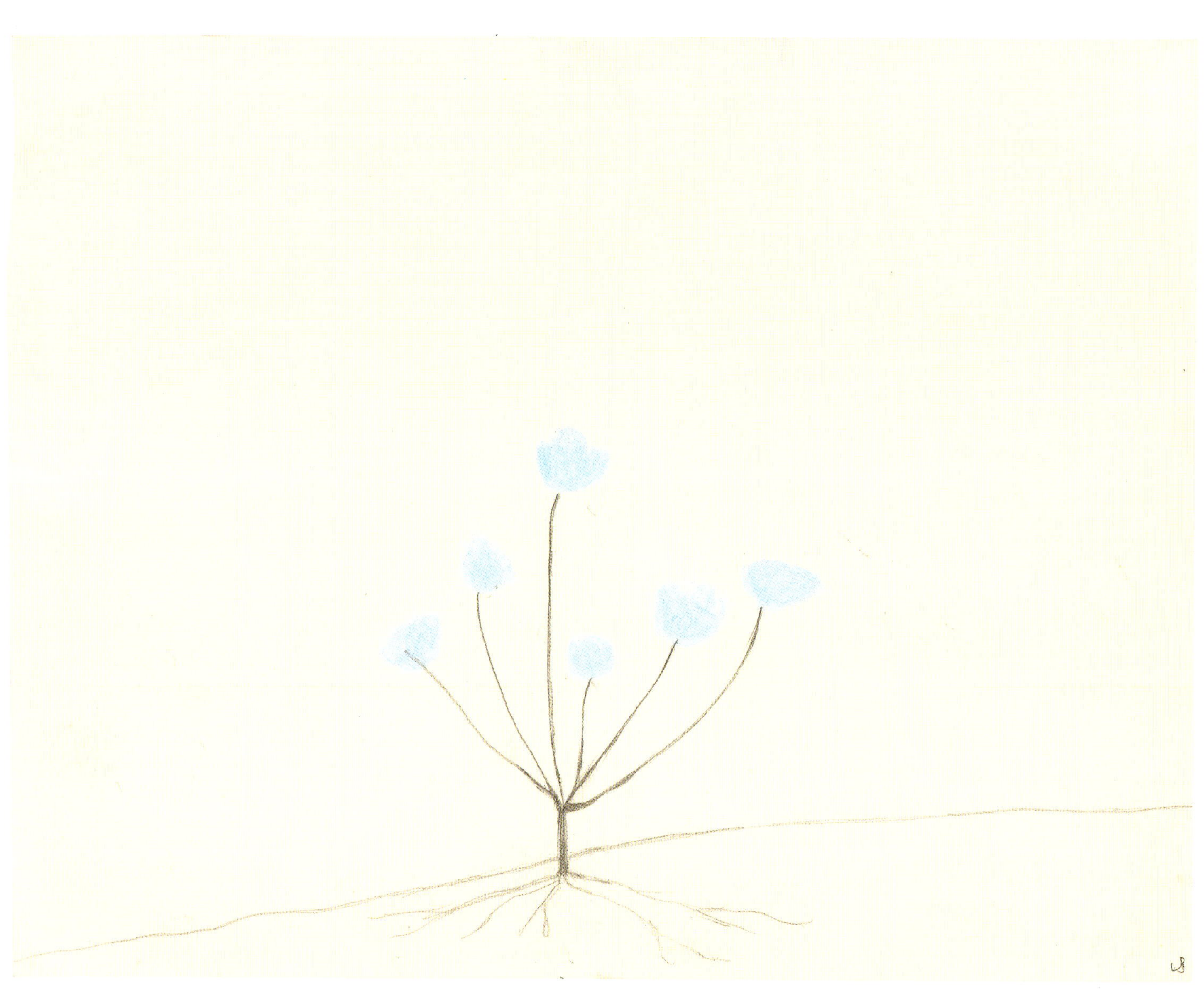

Ohne Titel/Untitled, 1997
Bleistift und blauer Pastellstift auf Papier/
Pencil and Blue Crayon on Paper, 23 x 30 cm

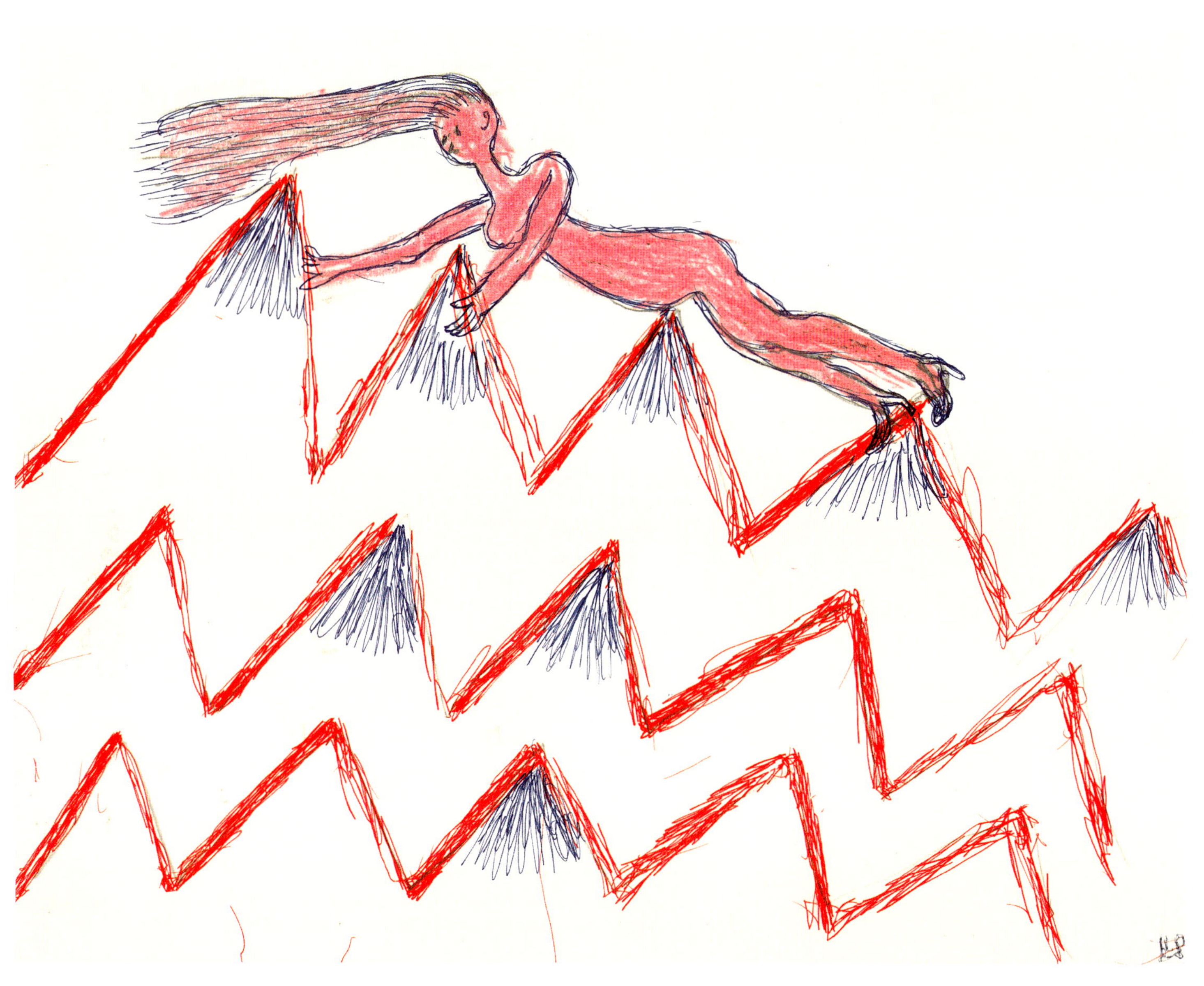

Miss Moody, 1998
Rote und blaue Tinte, rosa Pastellstift und Bleistift auf Papier/
Red and Blue Ink, Pink Crayon and Pencil on Paper, 23 x 30 cm o